Reconstructing Old Age

Reconstructing Old Age

New Agendas in Social Theory and Practice

Chris Phillipson

SAGE Publications
London • Thousand Oaks • New Delhi

First published 1998

 SAGE Publications Ltd
6 Bonhill Street
London EC2A 4PU

SAGE Publications Inc.
2455 Teller Road
Thousand Oaks, California 91320

SAGE Publications India Pvt Ltd
32, M-Block Market
Greater Kailash – I
New Delhi 110 048

British Library Cataloguing in Publication data

A catalogue record for this book is available
from the British Library

ISBN 0 8039 7988 6
ISBN 0 8039 7989 4 (pbk)

Library of Congress catalog card number 98–61237

Typeset by Photoprint, Torquay, Devon
Printed in Great Britain by Redwood Books, Trowbridge,
Wiltshire

CONTENTS

ACKNOWLEDGEMENTS

A large number of people have played a vital role during the writing of this book. I should first place on record my thanks to the University of Keele for the provision of periods of research leave. Without these it would certainly have been much more difficult both to write the book and to develop some of the arguments that are presented in the study. Many of these have drawn upon the writings of American gerontologists, and part of my research leave was spent in the USA where colleagues at the University of South Florida at Tampa provided a stimulating environment within which to reflect about the development of gerontology. I would like to express particular thanks to Jordan Kosberg, Juanita Garcia, Larry Mullins and Wiley Mangum, and the late Harold Sheppard. I would like here to acknowledge my own debt to the work of Harold Sheppard, whose writings on industrial gerontology were of great influence when I was studying for a PhD in the 1970s. He was a fine academic who engaged both with the politics as well as the sociology of ageing; he will be sorely missed on the gerontological scene. In relation to the USA, I must also acknowledge a broader debt to those working in the field of critical gerontology. As will be obvious from this book, I have been greatly inspired by the work of Carroll Estes and Meredith Minkler, and count as a very good fortune to have both as friends as well as colleagues. Their work has had a huge impact on the study of ageing over the past two decades.

The book has also benefited from many colleagues and friends in Britain. I have discussed many of the ideas at annual conferences organized by the British Society of Gerontology. The Society has been highly supportive to me over the years, and important in breaking through the isolation and doubts that inevitably accompany the writing of single-authored books. I have also drawn inspiration from being part of a strong gerontological team at Keele, and would like to acknowledge the help and encouragement of this group. I am grateful as well to Karen Phillips and Kiren Shoman at Sage for keeping faith with the writing of the book, despite many delays in producing the final manuscript. Sue Allingham worked hard and with great efficiency on various drafts of the typescript.

When my first book was written, it was dedicated to Jane, my partner. Sixteen years on the dedication remains the same, except that Jane is now my wife, and we have been joined by Isabel and Luke. Writing books certainly invades family life but in this case the family has been a major support and inspiration as well. I am enormously grateful for the help and encouragement which it has provided.

1

INTRODUCTION:
THE CRISIS OF SOCIAL AGEING

The impact of an ageing population has generated considerable debate over the past few years. This has emerged against a background of rapid change regarding the environment facing older people. The critical factors here have been: first, the growth in public awareness and interest in ageing issues; second, the crisis over pensions and the funding of the welfare state; third, the pressures on older people in the workplace combined with the rapid growth in early retirement.

Taken together, these changes represented a significant shift in the nature of discussions about old age during the 1980s and into the 1990s. In this period, old age entered a time of change and uncertainty. On the one hand, debates focused on the idea of growing old as a period of opportunity and liberation, in particular from restricted roles at work and within the family (Dychtwald, 1989). On the other hand, concern was expressed about the marginalization of older people, and the lack of meaning and purpose that seemed to characterize their daily lives (Cole, 1992; Moody, 1993).

An added focus to debates – initially in the USA but increasingly in the UK and elsewhere – has been expressed in the form of doubts about the terms of the intergenerational contract: were we providing older people with resources that would be unavailable to their children or their grandchildren? To what extent was an ageing population an unwelcome burden, a diversion from the more important task of feeding and educating children (Preston, 1984)? Was there a moral duty on the old to recognize that claims for expensive health care must be curtailed and controlled (Callahan, 1987)?

Such questions are, by any criteria, of major importance for western societies. They have become even more significant given a context of far-reaching changes to key social and economic relationships within these societies. Here, the argument from writers such as Anthony Giddens (1991) and Ulrich Beck (1992) is that we have entered a period of 'high' or 'advanced modernity'. The characteristics of this period include radical changes to industrial life (with the emergence of a post-industrial society); the impact of globalization; and the development of more fluid and pluralized forms of identity.[1] The uncertainties of old age are, thus, matched by major upheavals within western societies. It is the interplay between these elements which form the focus of this book. In particular, we are concerned to explore, on the one hand, the way in which old age has transformed many aspects of society; and on the other hand, the way in which ageing is itself being reshaped by dominant social, economic and political institutions.

Old age and the crisis of identity

The major argument of this book is that we have entered a period of crisis in respect of the identity of elderly people. The view developed is that old age has been shaped in two different ways in the post-war period. In the first period (mainly from the 1950s through to the early 1970s), emphasis was placed on the construction of old age around the institutions of retirement and the welfare state. These were seen as enabling the development of a secure old age, to be achieved through a combination of pensions from the state, and employment up to 60, 65 and beyond. Notwithstanding the manifest inadequacies of the welfare state (documented in studies such as Townsend's (1962) *The Last Refuge* and Abel-Smith and Townsend's (1965) *The Poor and the Poorest*), it was viewed as the crucial instrument for maintaining a sense of hope and purpose for elderly people.

By the 1970s and 1980s, however, this particular vision had begun to fray at the edges. The development of earlier retirement created new pressures in respect of financial support. Added to this, the era of unparalleled growth in the welfare state was abruptly halted in the mid-1970s. A combination of events – the rise in world oil prices, a slow-down in economic growth, combined with a simultaneous rise in unemployment and inflation – was to challenge basic assumptions about future spending on welfare (Armstrong et al., 1984; Phillipson and Walker, 1986; Glennerster and Hills, 1998).

By the 1990s, the unravelling of the system of retirement, along with changes to the welfare state, had begun to pose significant threats to elderly people. Both institutions have, it might be argued, suffered a crisis as regards their meaning and status within society. Retirement is no longer central – for increasing numbers of men and women – as a system organizing exit from the workplace (Kohli et al., 1991). Alongside this, the welfare state is increasingly undermined or 'residualized' in respect of providing care and support in periods such as old age (Walker, 1995). At one level, these changes have resulted in a language and ideology which scapegoats the old, defining them as a burden and cost to society (Bengston and Achenbaum, 1993; Walker, 1996). At a more individual level, however, they raise important existential issues about the nature and meaning of growing old.

The argument of this book is that we have in fact reached a historic turning point in the debate about the character and significance of ageing populations. The nature of demographic change has, of course, been a central concern throughout the twentieth century (Phillipson, 1982). Invariably, the focus has been on the 'costs' and 'burdens' attached to such change, rather than on the challenges and opportunities (Royal Commission on Population, 1949; DHSS, 1981). However, for at least a quarter of a century, following the end of the Second World War, anxieties were deflected by the tasks associated with maintaining a commitment to full employment, building the welfare state, and creating the basis for a secure retirement (Hill, 1993; Lowe, 1993; Clarke, 1996).

These activities were associated with a view that achieving a secure old age was a primary goal for society and the state. By the 1990s, however, some of the central pillars associated with this vision had been removed: first, the goal of full employment has long been abandoned, with older workers being one of the first groups to suffer the conse- quences. Second, the state retirement pension has come under increasing threat, with its de-indexation from wages leading to a steady loss in value (14 per cent of average male earnings in 1997; scheduled to fall to 9 per cent by 2020). Third, spending on the National Health Service has declined to a point where, according to some analysts, we may be at the beginning of the end of universal comprehensive health care, free at the point of use (Dilnot, *Guardian*, 23 January 1997). Fourth, what is termed as the 'intergenerational' contract is being questioned, with workers viewed as increasingly disinclined to pay tax increases to support improved services and benefits for groups such as older people (Thomson, 1996).

The focus of this study is on the implications of the crisis affecting each of these elements. However, the argument advanced is that the key issues are not solely concerned with, for example, the financial problems of older people, or with the provisioning of health services – despite the importance of both of these. Rather, the combined impact of the changes identified has been to place in doubt the meaning and purpose of growing old. For a period, retirement and the welfare state ensured a focus for the social construction of old age. Both were seen to contribute to the emerging identity associated with later life. Retirement had begun to provide a secure status for (in the USA) 'senior citizens' or for those entering what Laslett (1989) termed 'the third age'. Alternatively, for those inside what Featherstone and Hepworth (1989) were to describe as 'deep old age', the welfare state offered its own set of values and justification for being a very elderly person. However, with the foundations of both now removed, the location and meaning of old age has become uncertain. It is this development which is at the heart of the social crisis of ageing and which is the major focus of this book.

The task of this study is, therefore, to describe and analyse some of the major changes affecting the lives of older people. These will, however, be located within the context of particular theories, both within the field of social gerontology (the study of social aspects of ageing), and within sociology (the study of social relationships and institutions). Up until the late 1970s at least, social theory tended to play a marginal role in studies of ageing, a point made by Fennell et al. (1988) in their book *The Sociology of Old Age*. After this period, however, there was a substantial growth of interest in theorizing about growing old, with the development of what has been termed the 'political economy of ageing', or more broadly 'critical gerontology'. One of the aims of this study, therefore, is to review the literature which has developed in this area, and to assess the relevance of some of the arguments for understanding the changes affecting older people.

Besides theories drawn from within social gerontology, sociological theory itself has much to contribute. Again, one of the reasons for writing this book was to indicate the importance of a sociological perspective – for those studying old age, for those studying sociology, and, hopefully, for sociologists themselves. The discipline of sociology represents, then, an important framework for discussing and interpreting issues of concern both to older people, as well as to those researching and working with them. Some arguments in favour of using a sociological perspective will now be briefly summarized before being developed in greater detail in later chapters of this book.

The sociology of old age

An initial observation is that the sociology of old age still remains an undeveloped area in the UK. Despite the remarkable work of Peter Townsend in the 1950s and 1960s – and both *The Family Life of Old People* and *The Last Refuge* are classic works of sociology in this or any other period – the subsequent record has been a disappointing one. Certainly, in terms of the growth period of sociology, during the late 1960s through to the early 1980s, work in the sociology of old age was somewhat limited in terms of its theoretical content and empirical ambitions. In part, this was because of the strength of another tradition of enquiry – social policy and social administration. In this area, studies of, or including, older people have been firmly established in a line from Booth, Rowntree, Beveridge, Titmuss, Townsend and Wedderburn.[2] This tradition has been enormously creative both in terms of establishing the extent of poverty experienced by older people, and influencing government policy in areas such as pension reform, social security, and health and social policy (Walker, 1980).

Despite the importance and value of approaches drawn from social policy and social administration, the urgent need for new perspectives on old age was being highlighted from the late 1970s. The reasons for this are both general, and more specific, to the period under discussion. In respect of the former, a sociology of old age provides a different and necessary perspective about the issues facing older people. The sociologist starts from the view that old age is interesting because – although it is an enduring human phenomenon handled differently by different societies – it is changing and influencing social behaviour. The sociologist is concerned to explore the processes involved and how they are being interpreted by men and women. This approach contrasts with social policy and government interests in old age. In these contexts, old age is regarded as a problem (for the economy or the health service, for instance), hence the need for some analysis and collection of data. This approach has its own validity and justification but it leads to a distorted view of older people, together with a limited selection of topics to be analysed and discussed. It leads, in addition, to a focus on the weaknesses of older people, rather than on their strengths, together with an emphasis on their similarities rather than their differences (Fennell et al., 1988).

Sociological perspectives have an additional, more specific contribution to make, namely clarifying the nature of long-term social trends. The emergence of retirement is one example. This can be viewed as an economic problem – for the individual and for society – or as a psychological issue leading to problems of adjustment (Phillipson, 1993). However, retirement may also be seen as creating major changes in social relationships and activities. Earlier retirement, for example, is leading to a re-evaluation of the balance between work and leisure, with a greater emphasis on constructing a lifestyle which either combines elements of paid work with longer periods of leisure, or which focuses exclusively on recreational pursuits (Schuller and Bostyn, 1992).

These developments raise many important questions: will this trend stimulate yet further expansion in the service sector of the economy? Who will gain and who will lose as the period of time spent in full-time work contracts? What are the implications for the family? Will patterns of care change or remain the same as the work/leisure balance is changed? Will the household division of labour be modified, with some older men taking on a broader range of domestic and caring responsibilities (Laczko and Phillipson, 1991)? None of these questions can be

answered in the absence of a sociological perspective. Indeed, the fact
that they await answers (and are the subject of much confusion in policy
circles) reflects the present limitations in the sociology of old age. This
aspect is further reinforced by the nature of the debate about old age in
the 1980s and early 1990s. Here, there are two main points to consider:
first, the fiscal crisis in the welfare state has placed older people in the
spotlight as the main beneficiaries of public expenditure (Longman, 1987;
Johnson et al., 1989; Phillipson, 1990). Questions about the extent to
which the welfare state could be supported thus invariably raised issues
about the financing of care and support for older people.

Second, there was belated recognition in the 1980s and early 1990s of
the implications of demographic change. Despite the 1949 *Report* of the
Royal Commission on Population, and the 1954 Phillips Report (whose
estimate of a population of 9.5 million over pensionable age by 1979
was accurate to within a few thousand elders), governments expressed
surprise in the late 1970s and early 1980s at the extent of population
ageing. This was subsequently to be used as a justification for curtailing
public expenditure in general, and spending on older people in particular (Bornat et al., 1985).

On the one side, then, there has been concern about the financing of
the welfare state; on the other side, greater awareness about the extent of
the demographic shift which has taken place over the post-war period.
Both these developments have gone some way towards reawakening an
interest on the part of social scientists about issues relating to old age.
Given this, the concern here is to draw together a variety of arguments
which represent a sociological perspective on growing old. Inevitably, in
a book of this kind, the view presented will be somewhat partial and
selective. This is not a textbook on the sociology of old age, although
books such as those by Atchley (1994), Moody (1998), and Morgan and
Kunkel (1998) provide a useful complement to this study. Nor does it
provide a review of the health and social policy of old age in the usual
sense (the collection edited by Bernard and Phillips, 1997, is again
complementary). Rather, the concern here is to place the debates around
old age into particular theoretical frameworks on the one side, and
certain types of social change on the other.

In this context, the book builds upon an earlier book from the author,
Capitalism and the Construction of Old Age. This identified the case for
looking at old age as an experience which was shaped by the social
relations and institutions characteristic of a capitalist society. Four arguments were advanced for exploring the impact of capitalism on older
people (Phillipson, 1982: 3–5): first, whenever capitalism is in crisis – as
in the 1930s or in the early 1980s – it is inevitably working-class people
(especially those who become unemployed or are forced into retirement)
who suffer most. Indeed, what we see is an attempt by capitalism to

solve its problems through cuts in the living standards of working people. The expansion in, for example, the number of people entering early retirement may be seen as a thinly disguised attempt to reduce the social impact of unemployment. Many of those who retire early, once their 'golden handshakes' have been exhausted, experience many years of poverty, with no chance of re-entering the labour market except in the most menial of jobs. Certainly, in terms of the sacrifices which are constantly being urged upon working people, the price can be very high.

Second, capitalism has a distinct set of priorities which almost always relegates social and individual needs behind the search for profits. Third, as a social system capitalism can have a disastrous impact on the lives of older people. Through the decline of major industries, areas which were once prosperous fall into decay, creating sub-standard housing, loss of jobs, and the migration of younger workers with families (Community Development Projects, 1977). Elderly people find themselves caught in a 'scissors' between their own need for better services, and the steady decline of facilities within their neighbourhood.

Fourth, capitalism remains a system of exploitation: a ruling class still appropriates and controls the wealth produced by the working class. When the older worker steps permanently outside the wage system she or he becomes reliant on personal savings, an occupational pension or the basic state pension.

These conditions have changed in certain respects in the 15 years since the author's earlier book was written. But the form in which many people experience growing old age retains some crucial similarities: fears regarding poverty and loss of income; fears about the adequacy of provision for health care, fears about the use of time and leisure – all of these still affect the lives of millions of people at some point in their old age. Many changes have, of course, affected the lives of elderly people; some, perhaps many, gains have been made. But the argument of this book is that the experience of growing old is still disturbing and often alienating (to use a concept popular in the 1970s and one used by Gladys Elder (1977) – herself a pensioner – writing about old age in this period) for many individuals. The task of what follows is to provide analysis as well as answers to why this should still be the case.

Structure of the book

The book is divided into three parts: Part I develops a critical framework for interpreting some of the main changes affecting the lives of older people. Part II illustrates these taking three specific examples: the recon-struction of retirement; the crisis affecting the provision of pensions; the debate regarding intergenerational relationships. Part III develops the theoretical framework for interpreting some of the issues surround-ing the concern with population ageing, and also considers some issues relating to policy and practice.

The theme of each chapter is as follows: Chapter 2 reviews some of the key trends to emerge in critical gerontology over the past decade. This area has been a lively forum for the development of new perspectives on growing old, with a range of disciplines contributing to the debate. The chapter highlights some of the main contributions from scholars in Britain, the USA and elsewhere, with a summary of the strengths and limitations of particular theories.

Chapter 3 gives an overview of the dominant social and economic forces currently affecting retirement and growing old. The argument developed is that we have entered a period of destabilization in the way in which ageing is both experienced and constructed. The main institu-tions which once shaped the lives of older people are now under threat. The chapter examines the background to these changes and considers as well some of the pressures facing older people themselves.

Chapter 4 moves the argument on to analyse the nature of identity in what have been termed 'late modern' or 'postmodern' societies. The purpose here is to provide a theoretical framework for understanding the impact of the changes discussed in the second part of the book. This chapter draws on the writings of sociologists such as Anthony Giddens, Ulrich Beck and Zigmunt Bauman, as well as contributions from philos-ophers such as Charles Taylor. The second half of the chapter uses the work of these writers to explore ideas about the way in which the self is constructed in older age.

The next three chapters examine some of the key ways in which old age was destabilized during the 1980s and 1990s. Chapter 5 focuses on the issue of work and retirement, and the changes associated with the growth of early retirement. For a period of 30 years from 1950 to 1980, retirement grew and developed as a major stage in the life course. Associated with this was a significant shift in attitudes, from initial hostility on the part of (especially) working-class people, to positive acceptance of the benefits of retirement. After a period in the 1980s of rapid expansion in the numbers officially or unofficially defined as 'retired', concern began to be expressed that the high rates of retirement were no longer affordable. Increasingly, the view was expressed that an ageing population would require more older people to remain within paid employment. By the end of the 1990s, retirement had become a 'contested institution', with the development of policies – in the USA and in most European countries – aimed at delaying the exit of older people from work. This shift in views about older workers will be examined in this chapter, along with an assessment of the greater complexity associated with the transition from work to retirement.

Chapter 6 considers the history of pension provision, with a particular focus on the period since the Second World War. Again, we explore the complex shifts in trends over this period: the complacency after the founding of the welfare state, that poverty in old age had finally been conquered; the rediscovery of poverty in the 1960s; the 'golden age' of financial support for retirement in the early 1970s; the scandal over the selling of private pensions in the late 1980s and early 1990s; and the concern with the declining value of the basic state retirement pension which characterized virtually the whole of the 1990s (and which led to a major review of pensions being launched in 1997). These twists and turns in the history of pension provision signify that economic provision for old age has always reflected prevailing views about the state of the economy. Unfortunately, it seems rarely to have been the case that such views have been positive for a long enough period radically to alter the financial dependency of older people.

The final chapter in Part II examines the debate about inter-generational relations, with a sociological interpretation of the idea of conflict between workers and pensioners. The main arguments of the generational conflict position are reviewed, and the limitations of this perspective analysed. The conclusion drawn is that although conflict between age and generational groups is unlikely, the terms of the debate are symptomatic of a wider malaise about the status of old age. The idea of generations withdrawing support for older people may not have a sound empirical basis; it does, however, reflect a cultural unease about the way in which populations are changing, and uncertainty as to the extent to which this represents a positive or negative development.

Part III presents a broad overview of the main issues identified in the earlier parts of the book. Chapter 8 represents an historical and socio-logical interpretation of the changing fortunes of older people in the twentieth century. The chapter explores the evolution of what is termed the 'welfare self' and the 'retirement self' and the questioning of these discourses in the late twentieth century. The critique of these institutions has yet to generate, however, a clear alternative, hence the social and cultural vacuum which older people seemingly entered in the 1990s. This, it is argued, is raising considerable dangers and anxieties, these requiring an urgent response in respect of developing coherent social and economic policies.

Some suggestions for the basis of these is the subject of Chapter 9 of the book. This reviews arguments for reforms in particular areas (notably concerning pension and educational provision), but also considers some broader themes about the relationship between generations. There is then a brief concluding chapter summarizing the main themes and arguments presented in the book.

Writing about older age: two decades on

During the course of redrafting this book, I was struck by the differences and similarities between writing in 1997, and the period when my first book on old age was written – in the late 1970s and very early 1980s. Three issues perhaps stand out and it may be useful for the reader to know about these. First, writing in the late 1970s was vastly different at the very least because of the relatively limited range of studies then available. There was a substantial American literature, but very little from a critical perspective. Carroll Estes's (1979) *The Aging Enterprise*, which was to become highly influential in the 1980s, had yet to make its full impact. And significant papers by Walker (1981) and Townsend (1981) were still to be published. There was certainly no sense writing in Britain, say, in 1979 or even 1980, that a critical debate was about to unfold, one which would draw upon all the major disciplines from within the social sciences and the humanities.

The situation, writing in 1997, is certainly different. The publishing of critical and innovative texts on ageing continues apace, with notable contributions from Biggs (1993), Featherstone and Wernick (1995), Vincent (1995), Arber and Ginn (1996), Katz (1996), Quadagno and Street (1996), Minichiello et al. (1996), Jamieson et al. (1997), and Minkler and Estes (1998). These, and many other studies, represent a substantial intellectual framework within which it is possible to argue and debate the future of older age.

A second important contrast lies with older people themselves. Writing in the 1970s one had a relatively clear sense of who older people were: mainly poor, probably similar in outlook (and indeed appearance), and with limited aspirations for future lifestyles. This may have been an unsatisfactory stereotype then; it certainly must be considered as such now. Despite the trends and similarities to be identified in this study, there are huge variations among older people, and this diversity has undoubtedly been a feature of social change in the 1990s. Part of the aim of this book is, in fact, to give an account of this variation, as well as to consider the sociological implications. At the same time, the similarities in experience are important, and we shall probably say more about these in this study than is entirely satisfactory. There are major differences among older people, many of course related to factors associated with social class, gender and ethnicity. And the cumulative effects of biography are themselves significant, as the work of Thompson et al. (1990) has clearly demonstrated. But there are also common pressures which make it important to consider the meaning of old age in the twenty-first century: what is the impact on identity which accompanies the move into the last phase of the life course? In particular, what is the value of a sociological and critical perspective in trying to grapple with some of the changes affecting individuals in this period?

There is a final issue of great importance, and one which does in fact take us to the heart of the concerns of this study. It might be said that 20 years ago we were still dealing with a 'modernist' view of growing old, one which looked to the institutions of the state for supporting an ageing population. Now, we are more likely to relate to ageing as having all the complexities and hallmarks of a 'postmodern society': the range of lifestyles; the focus on individual choice; the more detached role of the state. At one level, the traditional space within which growing old was constructed has been undermined, most notably in relation to the organization of welfare. At another level, there appears to be a richer variety of possibilities for constructing old age and for being an older person. But the contrast is somewhat misleading. Labelling the new social ageing as 'postmodern' in fact raises complex questions about where old age has come from, and where precisely it is heading. Describing and explaining some of the characteristics of this journey forms much of the subject matter of this book.

Notes

1 For the reader needing a general introduction to the idea of 'postmodern societies', Kumar (1995) provides an excellent guide.

2 Bulmer et al. (1989) review the development of social policy as a discipline.

PART I

CRITICAL PERSPECTIVES

2

THE DEVELOPMENT OF CRITICAL GERONTOLOGY

In the 1990s, three important streams emerged in the growing debate about the nature of an ageing society. First, the continuation of political economy perspectives, this emerging from early work from Estes (1979), Walker (1981), Guillemard (1983), and others (see Minkler and Estes, 1991 and 1998; Phillipson, 1991; Estes, 1993, for reviews of this area).

Second, there is the work of researchers from the humanities, with important studies from scholars such as Thomas Cole, Harry Moody, Andrew Achenbaum and Andrew Wernick. Some of the main perspectives from this tradition were brought together in a number of volumes published in the early 1990s, these combining the research of historians, ethicists, and other scientists (see, especially, Cole et al., 1992; Cole et al., 1993; Schaie and Achenbaum, 1993; Bengston and Achenbaum, 1993).

Third, there is the emergence of biographical and narrative perspectives in gerontology, this building on the work of Malcolm Johnson (1976) and Jaber Gubrium (1986). Advocates of this approach have made important contributions to critical gerontology (see, for example, Gubrium, 1993), as well as extending our knowledge about the social construction of later life (Ruth and Kenyon, 1996a).

Taken together, these intellectual trends may be seen as illustrating the emergence of a critical as opposed to traditional gerontology (Phillipson and Walker, 1987; Baars, 1991). The critical elements in this gerontology centre around three main areas: first, from political economy, there is awareness of the structural pressures and constraints affecting older people, with divisions associated with class, gender and ethnicity being emphasized (Estes, 1993). Second, from both a humanistic as well as a biographically orientated gerontology, there is concern over the absence of meaning in the lives of older people, and the sense of doubt and uncertainty which is seen to pervade their daily routines and relationships (Moody, 1992). Third, from all three perspectives, comes a focus on the issue of empowerment, whether through the transformation of society (for example, through the redistribution of income and wealth), or the development of new rituals and symbols to facilitate changes through the life course (Kaminksy, 1993).

Critical gerontology in fact draws on a variety of intellectual traditions, these including: Marx's critique of political economy; the Frankfurt School (Adorno, Horkheimer and Marcuse), and more recent researchers from this tradition such as Jürgen Habermas (1971; Moody, 1992); psychoanalytic perspectives (Biggs, 1997); as well as contemporary sociological theorists such as Anthony Giddens (1991). These different approaches are used both to challenge traditional perspectives within gerontology, and to develop an alternative approach to understanding the process of growing old.

Central to the idea of a critical gerontology is the idea of ageing as a socially constructed event. In respect of political economy, this is seen to reflect the role of elements such as the state and economy in influencing the experience of ageing. In relation to the humanities, the role of the individual actively constructing his or her world is emphasized, with biographical approaches emphasizing an interplay between the self and society (Kenyon, 1996). The idea of *lives* as socially constructed is perhaps the key theme of critical gerontology, with different points of emphasis depending on the approach taken.

Despite the growth of critical perspectives, it is clear that several uncertainties need to be faced if the scope and ambitions of this approach are to be fully realized. The meaning of critical gerontology is itself somewhat evasive, with its construction around a variety of discourses within the humanities and social sciences (Green, 1993; Biggs, 1997). At its simplest, critical gerontology, as Baars (1991) puts it, is concerned with: '. . . a collection of questions, problems and analyses that have been excluded by established [mainstream gerontology]'. These vary from questions about the role of the state in the management of old age (Townsend, 1981), to issues about the purpose of growing old within the context of a postmodern life course (Cole, 1992).

The focus of this chapter is on identifying the range of theories and perspectives contained within critical perspectives. The chapter will conclude with an assessment of the progress in this field, especially in respect of extending our knowledge about the contemporary crisis facing older people in the developed world.

Disengagement theory and social gerontology

Critical gerontology must be seen, in part, as a response to the limitations of traditional theorizing in the study of old age. At least up until the 1960s, the dominant approach was to focus upon ageing as a problem arising from concerns and anxieties residing within the individual. The key theoretical ideas, developed by researchers such as Cavan et al. (1949) and Havighurst (1954), were built around concepts of individual 'adjustment', 'activity', and 'life satisfaction'. Lynott and Lynott argue here that:

> These concepts were to be understood to be a working language describing the central process of growing old. They were not part of a formal theoretical system whose major problem was whether or not it provides an adequate explanation of ageing. Rather, the concepts were treated as the 'facts' of growing old . . . [Ageing] was seen as a process whereby individuals – not social systems, structures of domination or ideologies – hope to alter themselves in some way to deal satisfactorily with their experiences. The problem was not retirement, poverty, ill health, and/or social isolation *per se*; these were the conditions, seemingly 'natural ones'. Being natural, they were accepted by the researchers as the way things were, the facts of elderly life. (1996: 750)

It was precisely the 'naturalness' of the concerns facing older people that came to be questioned from the 1970s onwards. Other theoretical perspectives had, of course, emerged to provide an account of the experience of old age. Disengagement theory (Cumming and Henry, 1961), for example, led the way in providing an account which related the changing needs of the individual to those of the social system. The theory was developed in the late 1950s by a group of gerontologists associated with the Committee on Human Development at the University of Chicago. The group included Havighurst, Neugarten, Cumming and Henry. The researchers considered that properly to understand old age, elderly people had to be studied within their own environments as opposed to hospitals or nursing homes. The environment selected was Kansas City, Missouri, a large metropolitan centre. Here, a panel of people aged 50 and over were chosen as subjects, and interviewed over a number of years. The theory of disengagement was derived from analyses of these interviews.

The central postulate of the theory has been summarized by Cumming and Henry as follows:

> Ageing is an inevitable mutual withdrawal or disengagement resulting in decreased interaction between the ageing person and others in the social system he belongs to. The process may be initiated by the individual or by others in the situation. The aged person may withdraw more markedly from

some classes of people while remaining relatively close to others. His withdrawal may be accompanied from the outset by an increased preoccupation
with himself; certain institutions in society may make the withdrawal easy for
him. When the ageing process is complete the equilibrium which existed
in middle life between the individual and his society has given way to a
new equilibrium characterized by a greater distance and an altered type of
relationship. (1961: 14)

A key assumption in the theory concerned the way in which what was
termed 'ego energy' declines with age. As the ageing process develops,
individuals were seen to become increasingly self-preoccupied and less
responsive to normative controls. The theory is predominantly a psychological one, although references to social components locate it within
functionalism in theory and conservatism in political ideology. The
sociological premise is that, since death occurs unpredictably and would
be socially disruptive if people 'died in harness', there is a functional
necessity to expel from work roles any older person with a statistically
higher risk of death.[1]

Disengagement theory, while heavily criticized by researchers, was of
considerable significance in developing theoretical debates around the
social dimension of ageing. Passuth and Bengston (1996) suggest that
it was the first formal theory that attempted to explore the relationship between individual and social aspects of ageing. Disengagement
theory also stimulated a range of complementary as well as alternative
theoretical approaches, these including: modernization theory (Cowgill
and Holmes, 1972); exchange theory (Dowd, 1975); life course perspectives (Neugarten and Hagestad, 1976); and age stratification theory (Riley
et al., 1972). Although challenging many core assumptions of the disengagement model, these theories furthered the debate about the experience of growing old, applying in the process central concepts from
within the social sciences.[2]

Disengagement theory had a third, and possibly more significant,
impact on debates about ageing. For many researchers, conventional
theorizing in gerontology itself became part of the research problem.
Gerontological research – in its traditional form – was seen to be
colluding with a repressive and intolerant society (an issue raised by
social activists such as Maggie Kuhn). The concept of disengagement could be viewed, it was argued, as legitimating a form of social
redundancy among the old. Zena Blau, an American sociologist, drew
support from older people as well as researchers when she argued that:

The disengagement theory deserves to be publicly attacked, because it can so
easily be used as a rationale by the non-old, who constitute the 'normals' in
society, to avoid confronting and dealing with the issue of old people's
marginality and rolelessness in American society. (1973: 152)

It was precisely the concern identified by Blau which suggested the need for a different kind of gerontology. Traditionally, theory in social gerontology had avoided questioning the social problems and conditions facing older people, a point made by Carroll Estes in her seminal book *The Aging Enterprise*. By the 1970s, however, this came to be questioned in a context of political radicalization and economic recession. The result was the emergence of a different – critical – gerontology, one initially built around ideas drawn from Marxist political economy. The next section of this chapter identifies some influences on this approach and the key arguments advanced by its proponents.

The rise of political economy

The political economy perspective developed in the context of the crisis affecting public expenditure from the mid-1970s onwards (Phillipson and Walker, 1986). Traditional perspectives in gerontology had operated on the assumption of continued growth in state expenditure in areas such as pensions and welfare. The basis for this was undermined, however, with the rise in unemployment and inflation during the 1970s. Alongside this economic collapse was a significant political and economic change, with cuts to public expenditure in general and welfare spending in particular. Given that a substantial proportion of social expenditure was allocated to older people (Myles, 1984), they were inevitably subject to a sustained political attack by right-wing governments in Britain, the USA and elsewhere. This was to bring a significant change in perceptions about older people. The post-war vision of services to the elderly, as a crucial element of citizenship, now faced a significant challenge. Older people came to be viewed as a burden on western economies, with demographic change, especially the declining ratio of younger to older persons, seen as creating intolerable pressures on public expenditure.

A critical response to this crisis came from a number of studies that used a broad political economy approach. These included: *The Aging Enterprise* by Carroll Estes (1979); 'The Structured Dependency of the Elderly' by Peter Townsend (1981); 'Towards a Political Economy of Old Age' by Alan Walker (1981); *Political Economy, Health and Aging* by Estes et al. (1984); *Old Age in the Welfare State* by John Myles (1984); and *Capitalism and the Construction of Old Age* by the present author (1982).

A major concern of these studies was to challenge a view of growing old as a period dominated by physical and mental decline, an approach labelled as the biomedical model of ageing. This model was attacked for its association of age with disease, as well as for the way that it individualized and medicalized the ageing process (Estes and Binney, 1989). The alternative approach taken was to view old age as a social rather than biologically constructed status. In the light of this, many of the experiences affecting older people could be seen as a product of a particular division of labour and structure of inequality, rather than a natural part of the ageing process. Alan Walker (1981) developed this perspective with his concept of the 'social creation of dependency' in old age, and Peter Townsend (1981) used a similar term when he described the 'structured dependency' of older people. This dependency was seen to be the consequence of the forced exclusion of older people from work, the experience of poverty, institutionalization, and restricted domestic and community roles. Finally, Carroll Estes (1979: 2) introduced the term the 'ageing enterprise': '. . . to call particular attention to how the aged are often processed and treated as a commodity in our society and to the fact that the age-segregated policies that fuel the ageing enterprise are socially-divisive "solutions" that single-out, stigmatize, and isolate the aged from the rest of society'.[3]

The basic tenets of the political economy model have been defined in terms of developing 'an understanding of the character and significance of variations in the treatment of the aged, and to relate these to polity, economy and society in advanced capitalism' (Estes, 1986). Political economy has challenged the idea of older people being a homogeneous group unaffected by the dominant structures and ideologies within society. Instead, the focus is on understanding the relationship between ageing and economic life, the differential experience of ageing according to social class, gender and ethnicity, and the role played by social policy in contributing to the dependent status of older people (Minkler and Estes, 1998). Political economy also gives central consideration to the role of the state as an active force in managing the relationship between the individual and society. Estes (1998: 20) argues that the study of the state is fundamental to understanding old age for three main reasons: first, it has the power to allocate and distribute scarce resources; second, to mediate between the different segments and classes of society; third, to ameliorate conditions that threaten the social order. These activities have, as we shall see, been crucial in the construction of old age, with different points of emphasis over the course of the twentieth century.

The political economy perspective has been applied to a variety of concerns within the field of ageing. First, Graebner, Phillipson and Guillemard used this approach to examine the institutionalization of retirement (see Chapter 5). The retirement experience, its timing and eventual outcome were related to the supply and demand for labour and the production relations of a capitalist society. The growth of state pension schemes was itself related to economic factors, with, for example, the experience of mass unemployment being a stimulus behind legislation in countries such as the USA and Britain.

Second, the political economy model was significant in developing a range of counter-arguments to perceptions of demographic change as a cause of the state's fiscal crisis. Blaming older people was seen as a means of obscuring '. . . the origins of problems [which stem] from the capitalist economic system and the subsequent political choices that are made' (Estes, 1986: 123). Attacks on the burden of the elderly population were seen to legitimize a transfer of responsibilities from the state to individual older persons. At the same time, the class basis of old age policies meant that inequalities were not only maintained but were in fact widened through the encouragement of privatization in areas such as health care and financial support (Estes et al., 1996).

Third, the political economy approach also contributed, as already indicated, to theorizing about the relationship between age, race, class and gender (Estes, 1991; Minkler, 1996). This helped to produce a range of new questions for social gerontologists to explore. For example: how does the individual's lifelong identity change (if at all) with retirement? Are there specific transformations in respect of class and occupational identities? If so, what implications might this have for a political sociology of ageing?

Finally, political economy also provided a critical analysis of the character of health and social services. These were seen to reinforce the dependency created through the wider economic and social system. Welfare services were criticized for stigmatizing older people, compounding their problems through the imposition of age-segregated policies (Estes, 1979; 1993). In practical terms this analysis raised issues about challenging older people's experience of being passive consumers of welfare and medical services. It also raised questions about the relationship of professionals to older people: how far do they challenge the low expectations that elderly people have about services? To what extent do they contribute to the experience of old age as a period of dependency.

The critique of political economy

The political economy perspective is still being developed in a variety of ways by its original proponents (see, for example, Estes et al., 1996; Minkler and Estes, 1998). At the same time, a number of important criticisms have been made of this approach. Three in particular may be highlighted. First, an important concept developed in the theory is the idea of 'structured dependency' (Townsend, 1981; 1986). This draws attention to the way in which social and economic relations foster passivity in old age. At the heart of this process is the role of the state as a system of control and domination. Accordingly:

> The approach is one whereby society is held to create the framework of institutions and rules within which the general problem of the elderly emerge or, indeed, are 'manufactured'. In the everyday management of the economy and the administration and development of social institutions the position of the elderly is subtly shaped and changed. The policies which determine the conditions and welfare of the elderly are not just the reactive policies represented by the statutory social services but the much more generalised and institutionalised policies of the state which maintain or change social structure. (Townsend, 1986: 2)

This leaves unclear, however, the link between structures at a macro-sociological level, and individual behaviour and action. In this sense, structured dependency could be said to be over-deterministic in its approach, failing to address the way in which individuals could themselves challenge the impact of different forms of institutional control (Giddens, 1991; Bury, 1995).

Second, political economy has been charged with failing properly to address issues of gender. Bury (1995), for example, points out that the problems experienced by men and women do not arise solely through the operation of the labour market, but are 'part of a set of culture-bound gendered relationships' (Bury, 1995: 20). Political economy has, it is argued, underplayed the impact of gender differences in status and power and, as well, the effects of the cumulative oppression faced by women. This argument almost certainly carries more weight in the UK than the USA, where these issues have been more comprehensively addressed (see, for example, Arendell and Estes, 1991; Ovrebo and Minkler, 1993; Calasanti and Zajicek, 1993; Calasanti, 1996; Ray, 1996). On the other hand, the failure in Britain may be less the problem of the political economy of old age, and rather more the limitations of socio-logical work in general in dealing with gender inequalities in old age (the study by Arber and Ginn, 1991, is a notable exception here).

Third, political economy has been vulnerable to the charge of ignoring broader issues of meaning and purpose in the lives of the old. Focusing on questions of structure has tended to sideline, it is argued, the important moral and existential issues faced by older people. These areas have certainly been more central to the tradition of theorizing represented in the humanities. On the other hand, wider concerns have been explored in debates around generational equity (see Chapter 7), where the idea of interdependency between generations has been a major theme in political economy perspectives (Walker, 1996; Phillipson, 1996; Minkler, 1996).

Despite the above criticisms, political economy has continued to play an important (and subversive) role in monitoring and explaining structural changes in the welfare state. It has also been pivotal in challenging the 'alarmist' or 'apocalyptic' demography which has become common-place in the 1990s (Robertson, 1998). This development raised a new set of concerns around both societal attitudes and cultural assumptions about the position of older people – what has been termed the 'moral economy of ageing' (Minkler and Cole, 1998). Awareness of the moral dimension to growing old has become an important issue both within political economy and through the influence of work from within the humanities. An assessment of some of the arguments from this latter perspective will now be considered.[4]

The crisis of meaning

The approach taken by political economy highlighted the role of the state and capital in the construction of ageing as a demographic crisis. Another response has been to locate problems of ageing within a broader paradigm, one linked to the limitations both of western culture and positivistic social and natural sciences. The former has been addressed by Thomas Cole (1992), in his book *The Journey of Life: A Cultural History of Aging in America*. In this study, Cole traces what he sees as the historical shift from viewing ageing as an existential problem, to one focused around scientific and technical management. Cole argues:

> By the early twentieth century, ageing had been largely cut loose from earlier religious, cosmological, and iconographic moorings, made available for modern scientific enquiry. Laboratory scientists and research physicians attempted to cast off religious dogma and mystery surrounding natural processes. Rejecting transcendental norms and metaphysical explanations, they turned to biology in the hope that nature itself contained authoritative ideas and explanations of old age. (1992: 192–4)

Cole argues that ultimately this has proved a dangerous illusion in respect of understanding the nature of ageing. Scientific enquiry cannot replace, he argues, the essential mystery and 'fatedness of the course of life'. By presenting ageing as a technical problem, we have lost sight of the fact that it is 'biographical as well as biological'; that 'old age is an experience to be lived meaningfully and not only a problem of health and disease'. Cole concludes that:

> We must acknowledge that our great progress in the material and physical conditions of life has been achieved at a high spiritual and ethical price. Social security has not enhanced ontological security or dignity in old age. The elderly continue to occupy an inferior status in the moral community marginalized by

an economy and culture committed to the scientific management of growth without limit. (1992: 237)

This position has also been developed by Harry Moody (1988; 1992; 1993), in a series of papers drawing out the implications of a humanistic approach to the study of ageing. Moody is concerned with the development of a critical gerontology that breaks from the positivist tradition, and which acknowledges the central place of meaning and interpretation in the construction of social life. For Moody, the abstract language of social science and the ordinary language of daily experience are tied in ways that demand explication or interpretation. There are no straightforward 'facts', in other words, about social ageing. Moody (1988: 32) illustrates this point by taking what seems to be the 'deceptively simple question: What is it that constitutes retirement? How do we know, for example, how many people are retired at any given time or how retirement behaviour has changed over time?' Moody suggests that answering such questions is somewhat complex, because:

> to some extent *retirement* is a shared meaning of social events, an interpretation of *why* an individual no longer participates in the paid labour force. One and the same individual may have been laid off or be partially disabled and may then describe him or herself to a survey researcher as 'retired', whereas others might describe the individual as 'unemployed' . . . The failure of researchers to acknowledge the preinterpreted world is no innocent error. The uncritical acceptance of retirement rates as an unambiguous 'fact' about the social world becomes a kind of mystification of the lived experience of unemployment and chronic illness, and this mystification has political as well as ideological consequences. (1988: 32)

Moody's development of a critical gerontology is to define it against what he sees as its opposite, namely, that of *instrumental gerontology*. This he views as the province of conventional social science, where the emphasis is upon the development of new tools to predict and control human behaviour. Social gerontology, according to this view, is dominated by a form of rationality that seeks to objectify what is essentially a human and subjective experience. Instrumental reason forces us to stand outside ageing as an individual process, suggesting that it can be controlled through a variety of technical interventions. To set against this, the task of a critical gerontology is to reinsert the notion of ageing as a 'lived experience', one which demands a dialogue between the older person, the academic community, practitioners, and other relevant groups. Moody suggests, however, that critical gerontology must go beyond merely a negative critique of current practice and ideology, offering as well its own vision of a different approach. Accordingly:

> A critical gerontology must also offer a positive idea of human development: that is, ageing as movement toward freedom beyond domination (autonomy,

wisdom, transcendence). Without this emancipatory discourse (i.e. an expanded image of ageing) we have no means to orient ourselves in struggling against current forms of domination. (1988: 32–3)

Moody calls in fact for an emancipatory praxis (or practice) which can transcend the conventional categories of work, sex roles and age stereotypes. These are seen to circumscribe the possibilities of human development, and to produce a 'shrunken and fragmented view of what the life course might be' (Moody, 1988: 35).

Subjectivity and social research

The concern to 'reinsert' human subjectivity into the study of ageing has prompted several important developments – notably with the encouragement of qualitative and interpretive methods in ageing research. Two examples illustrate this theme: first, the interest in biographical perspectives in the study of ageing; second, the influence of a phenomenologically orientated sociology.

Biographical perspectives have an extensive pedigree in the social sciences, with notable examples including: the symbolic interactionist approach of the Chicago School (Blumer, 1969), and the work of sociologists of the life course such as Thomas and Znaniecki (1966). Johnson (1976), drawing on sociologists such as Erving Goffman and Howard Becker, developed the notion of ageing as a 'biographical career'. He put forward the case for 'reconstructing biographies' in order to identify the development of life histories, and the way that these have 'sculpted present problems and concerns' (Johnson, 1976; see also Thompson et al., 1990). Ruth and Kenyon (1996a) note the influence of Bertaux's volume *Biography and Society: The Life History Approach in the Social Sciences*, this identifying the importance of using biography as a methodological approach within social research.

Subsequently, the biographical perspective was extended by researchers such as Coleman, Birren, Ruth and Kenyon, with the key arguments brought together in a collection edited by Birren et al. (1996) entitled *Aging and Biography*. The view adopted was that biographical approaches can contribute towards understanding both individual and shared aspects of ageing over the life course. Examining reactions to personal crises and turning points could provide researchers with unique insights into the way individuals construct their lives. Equally, however, studying lives provides a perspective on the influence of social institutions such as work and the family. Biographical data thus helps us to understand what Ruth and Kenyon (1996b) refer to as the possibilities and limits set by the historical period in which people live.

Ruth and Kenyon (1996b) summarize the value of using biographical materials as threefold: first, at a general level, they contribute to the development of theories of adult development and ageing; second, they provide a focus on both the public and the personal way in which lives develop; third, they are important in determining ways to enhance the quality of life. Central to the biographical approach is the idea of the 'reflexivity' of the self, or the way in which individuals both influence the world around them, while modifying their own behaviour in response to information from this world. This idea (which strongly parallels the sociology of the self developed by Giddens, 1991, and others) leads to a view that focuses on a 'responsive' and 'changing self'. Ruth and Kenyon emphasize this point in the following way:

> A potentially optimistic feature of viewing human ageing biographically is that there is an openness or flexibility to the human journey . . . While there is continuity, there is also change and the possibility for change. In other words, there may be no necessary connection between the events of our lives, our number of years, and the meaning ascribed to those events; stories can be re-written, plots altered, and the metaphors traded in and traded up . . . according to the needs of the self. (1996b: 6)

As this quotation suggests, narratives or stories are seen to play a central role in the construction of lives. We express what is meaningful about ourselves through the telling of stories.[5] Story-telling is of importance in a wider cultural sense, hence the importance of oral history as a method of communicating the significance of particular lives and communities for society as a whole (the work of Thompson and Bertaux best illustrates this point).

At an individual level, however, the telling of stories is a medium for the integration of lives; for explaining discontinuities as well as continuities. Talking to people about the story of their lives (their 'auto-biographies') gives the researcher access to the way in which people 'age from within' (Ruth and Kenyon, 1996b). Invariably, this provides us with a different perspective to that of traditional gerontology, where the physical and social changes accompanying ageing are seen as the primary forces influencing the individual. Against this, researchers such as Kaufman present a more challenging view of the self:

> The old Americans I studied do not perceive meaning in ageing itself; rather, they perceive meaning in being themselves in old age . . . When old people talk about themselves, they express a sense of self that is ageless – an identity that maintains continuity despite the physical and social changes that come with old age. (1986: 6–7)

The emphasis on stories and narratives is especially prominent in the work of the American sociologist Jaber Gubrium (1993). Gubrium is concerned with, as he puts it, 'the manner by which experience is given voice'. He argues that while a focus on individual thoughts and feelings is important, the context in which these arise must also be studied. Context is being used here to refer to the way in which people both share and develop their own ideas about growing old, and the settings in which meanings are assigned. Gubrium (1993) argues, for example, that we should pay attention to how respondents raise and explore their own questions in response to those of the interviewer. Rather than dismiss their conjectures as so much research debris, the process itself identifies important issues about the construction of ageing:

> When a respondent states that his or her feelings or thoughts about something 'depends', I pay as much attention to the 'what' it depends on and the 'how' of the connection as to the eventual answer. When someone asks me what I mean by a particular question, I believe it important to zero in on how that meaning is mutually worked out. When a respondent states or marks that she both agrees and disagrees with a particular questionnaire item . . . it is important to probe how a single question can have a seemingly contradictory response. Rather than treat the response as methodologically meaningless, I wonder what kinds of questions could make such ostensible contradictions reasonable. (1993: 49)

Gubrium's work acknowledges two important issues about the social reality of ageing: first, certain aspects of ageing remain uncharted and ambiguous for many (if not all) individuals: researchers as well as elderly respondents have in this context the task of working out and reflecting upon the meaning of this stage in the life course. Second, it is also the case that many situations that affect older individuals (or their carers) are literally beyond their experience, thus creating complexities in terms of naming and identifying feelings and beliefs.[6] Much of Gubrium's work has focused on the issue of Alzheimer's disease, examining the way in which the meaning of the illness is derived and communicated. He uses the example of support groups for people with Alzheimer's to show the way in which these can provide a basis for speaking about and interpreting the caregiving experience. For Gubrium (borrowing a concept from social anthropology), the 'local cultures' of residential settings, day centres and support groups will provide important contexts for working through and assigning meanings to particular experiences. In this approach, language is seen to play a crucial role in the construction of reality. Lynott and Lynott make this point as follows:

> Instead of asking how things like age cohorts, life stages, or system needs organise and determine one's experiences, the phenomenologists turn the question around and ask how persons (professional and lay alike) make use of age-related explanations and justifications in their treatment and interaction with one another . . . Facts virtually come to life in their assertion, invocation, realization and utility. From this point of view, language is not just a vehicle for symbolically representing realities; its usage, in the practical realities of everyday life, is concretely productive of the realities. (1996: 754)

Gubrium (with Wallace, 1990) draws out an important and somewhat subversive conclusion from this fact, namely, that 'ordinary theorizing' (for example by older people themselves) should have equal (complementary status) to that of professionals. People are not merely *respondents* in the passive sense of the term; they develop facts and theories of their own, and the relevance of these deserves wider recognition. Using the standpoint of social phenomenology derived from Schutz and Husserl, Gubrium and Wallace argue that:

> When we suspend the natural attitude and allow the ordinary theoretical activity of the aged and others to become visible, a whole world of reasoning about the meaning of growing old . . . comes forth. We find that theory is not something exclusively engaged in by scientists. Rather there seem to be two existing worlds of theory in human experience, one engaged by those who live the experiences under consideration, and one organised by those who make it their professional business systematically to examine experience. To the extent we all attend to experience and attempt to understand it or come to terms with its varied conditions, we all theorise age. To privilege scientific theorising simply on the basis of its professional status makes scientistic what otherwise could be firm recognition of the theoretical activity of ordinary men and women, along with the opportunity to refocus social gerontology from behaviours to meanings embedded in ordinary discourse. (1990: 147)

The different perspectives discussed in this section take as their standpoint the centrality of the human subject in defining the social world of ageing. Through the medium of language, people describe the story or stories which make up their lives. Attention to these gives the researcher access not just to how particular individuals experience growing old, but also to the way in which ageing is constructed. Such a view provides a powerful corrective to the tendency – dominant in traditional gerontology – of seeing older people as 'empty vessels', reacting to, rather than shaping, experiences in later life. Taken together, however, the focus on meaning provided by humanistic gerontology and biographical perspectives on ageing have a number of limitations. The nature of these will now be discussed and summarized.

Constructing later life

There are at least three main problems which can be cited, shared to different degrees by both humanistic and biographical perspectives within gerontology. First, an important theme running through the biographical approach is that of the self actively constructing his or her social universe. However, the view of the self is inconsistent in the literature. At one extreme is Johnson's (1976) notion of the biographical career, in which the self would seem to be largely derived from the different strands making up a person's life. At the other extreme is the idea of the 'storied self', in which the underlying plot is open to endless revision. Although Kenyon (1996) denies the charge of solipsism, arguing for what he sees as the 'fundamental interpersonal dimension', the approach to the self seems at times somewhat too literal and open-ended. In particular, there is insufficient acknowledgement in this approach that social and structural constraints may compromise both biographical development and interaction with significant others in the universe of the older person.

A second problem concerns the extent to which social inequalities are taken into account in the subjective approach. Gubrium (1993), for example, makes a powerful case for a social gerontology which avoids 'privileging certain voices and silencing others'. But this assumes that professional researchers are able to overcome forms of oppression which themselves penetrate the language and relationships around which daily life is constructed. Assuming the methodological stance suggested by Gubrium may be effective for certain groups, less so for others. For certain Black-African or Asian groups, the experience of exclusion may compromise even explicit attempts to foreground all, rather than particular, voices of ageing.

Third, the work of Moody and Cole, in providing a critique of instrumental reason, seeks to demonstrate the way in which existing explanations of ageing are linked to forms of social control. Instrumental reason is seen to reify or mystify structures of social domination, thus reinforcing the status quo. As a formal critique, the arguments advanced are of considerable power. But the alternatives produced seem to lack substance. Moody refers to the need for 'emancipation', and for a 'positive vision of how the social order might be different' (1992: 295). But the form of the emancipation and the nature of a new social order is left unclear. Of course, the response might be that it must be left to those growing old themselves to define a different type of adult development, one which (in Cole's terms) would recover a sense of 'mystery' about the last phase in the life course. However, specifying the basis for emancipation would seem to be important and cannot be left entirely open-ended.

Conclusion

As the above review suggests, a number of strands may be identified within the broad area of critical gerontology. All may be seen as providing a valuable contribution to the debate about the way in which older age is socially constructed. As suggested, political economy has played a central role in highlighting structural inequalities within later life, and has challenged the specific form of crisis construction influencing the debate on ageing populations. Humanistic gerontology has advanced understanding about the experience of ageing as part of the whole course of life. At the same time, it has challenged the way in which older people have been marginalized within society, emphasizing the extent to which life appears emptied of meaning and significance. Finally, biographical perspectives draw out the importance of ways of coping and managing which have been formed over the life course. Placing the individual within the context of a particular life history is viewed as central for understanding how individuals adapt and respond to change in old age.

These different ideas and tendencies within gerontology will be used as a basis for exploring changes in the social construction of later life. We shall use these theories as tools for illuminating some of the contradictions and conflicts experienced by older people in their daily lives. The next two chapters build upon the theories reviewed in this chapter by examining in more detail the nature of this social construction. The task of the next chapter is to examine this through the policies and practices towards older people which developed after the Second World War, a time when western society identified old age as a time for a range of interventions in the field of economic and social policy.

Notes

1 Fennell et al. (1988) summarize some of the literature on disengagement theory. Hochschild's (1975) article remains one of the most incisive critiques of the theory.

2 Lynott and Lynott (1996) provide an excellent account of theoretical issues in the sociology of ageing.

3 See Estes (1993) for an examination of the approach taken in this book.

4 The critical reaction to studies such as Callahan's (1987) *Setting Limits*, was also influential in the development of the moral economy approach.

5 See McLeod (1997) for a valuable discussion of biographical and narrative perspectives as applied to the counselling field.

6 Grant (1998) explores this aspect in her powerful account of her mother's experience of dementia.

3

CONSTRUCTING OLD AGE

The previous chapter identified the variety of ways in which critical gerontology has analysed the experience of growing old. The theories discussed make significant contributions – from different vantage points – to furthering our understanding of the challenges that face people as they move through the life course. The various strands of critical gerontology indicate the combination of structural and biographical elements which influence identity in later life. Ageing, from this perspective, represents an interweaving of public and private lives, this creating much diversity in the experiences and lifestyles of older people.

Awareness of continuity and discontinuity in the lives of the old needs, however, to be complemented by a stronger sense of the historical and sociological forces that are changing (and often undermining) identities in later life. Critical gerontology, in fact, is built upon a number of assumptions about the nature of social change, in particular that which concerns the shift from a modern to a 'late' or 'postmodern' age. The purpose of this chapter is to outline some of the characteristics of the 'modernization' of ageing in the twentieth century. The destabilization of these elements, and the subsequent impact on the social position and identity of older people, is then explored in a variety of ways in the remaining chapters of this book.

Science and ageing

The starting point for our discussion concerns the period within which gerontology was developed as a subject of scientific interest and investigation. In both Europe and the USA, it was the 1940s that was the crucial 'take-off' period for the growth of research, the period after the ending of the Second World War being of particular importance (Amann, 1984; Birren, 1996). The background here concerns the influence of two factors: first, greater awareness about the significance of long-term population trends (highlighted in the UK in the report in 1949 of the Royal Commission on Population); second, the economic pressures prevailing in the aftermath of war, these leading to concerns about controlling the costs associated with population ageing.

The late 1940s and early 1950s were, then, crucial for the development and organization of research into ageing. The Gerontological Society of America was founded in 1945, with the American Geriatric Society being formed around the same time. The International Association of Gerontology (IAG) held its first meeting (in Belgium) in 1948, with a second congress in the USA (in St Louis) in 1951. The first Pan American Congress of Gerontology was held in Mexico City in 1956 (Birren, 1996).

In Britain, the Second World War had led, through the work of the Emergency Medical Service, to a 're-discovery of the plight of the chronically ill aged in under-served and under-resourced municipal hospitals and infirmaries' (Carboni, 1982: 76; Means and Smith, 1995). In addition, the development of the National Health Service provided financial and administrative support for the growth of geriatric medicine (Brockelhurst, 1978; Grimley-Evans, 1997). Applicants for the new consultant posts were also available. Carboni (1982), for example, notes the return to Britain of large numbers of consultants who were seeking new positions, but who faced a shortage of consultancies in the traditional medical specialties. Reflecting these developments, the Medical Society for the Care of the Elderly (later to become the British Geriatric Society) was formed in 1947.[1] Seven years later, the IAG held its third congress in London, producing what was to become an influential volume of proceedings from the congress, published in 1954 (International Association of Gerontology, 1954).

Books and research monographs soon followed these organizational developments. In the USA, the fruits of research were brought together in two major reference books on ageing: *The Handbook of Aging and the Individual: Psychological and Biological Aspects*, edited by James Birren (1959); and *The Handbook of Social Gerontology: Societal Aspects of Aging*, edited by Clark Tibbitts (1960). These were complemented by a third volume edited by Ernest Burgess (1960), which explored trends and developments in ageing in a number of western countries: *Aging in Western Societies: A Survey of Social Gerontology*.

This trilogy set out the structure and range of issues encompassing the field of ageing. Its importance was in identifying an ambitious programme for tackling the social and medical concerns arising from demographic change. This was to be achieved, first, through the foundation of university-based research centres (a particular feature in the USA); and second, through the fostering of collaboration from a range of academic disciplines. As Lawrence Frank expressed it in the first issue of the *Journal of Gerontology*:

> Gerontology is an enterprise calling for many and diversified studies, for pooled and concerted investigations, indeed, for the orchestration of all relevant disciplines and professional practices. (cited in Achenbaum, 1995: 125)

There was, in fact, a substantial growth in the development of research from the early 1950s. Writing in 1963, Clark Tibbitts concluded that half the scientific knowledge gained about ageing had been accumulated over the previous decade (cited in Achenbaum, 1995: 251). Birren and Clayton (1975) estimated that the literature on ageing published between 1950 and 1960 equalled all of that published in the preceding 115 years.

The research endeavour was shaped, however, by an important set of assumptions concerning the nature of ageing as a scientific and social enterprise. The 'discovery' of ageing as a social and medical problem coincided with what may be seen as the final phase in the development of modernity in western societies. Modernity here is taken as referring to the process of change, beginning in the sixteenth century and culminating in the nineteenth century, with the transformation of the western world from a mainly peasant to a predominantly urban and industrial society.

The general outline of modernity has been summarized by Leonard as follows:

> Modernity as a historical period in Western culture may be seen as having its origins in the 'Age of Enlightenment' which began towards the end of the eighteenth century. The historical trajectory from these origins to the present (or possibly recent past) may be understood as having been founded intellectually on a belief in the power of reason over ignorance, order over disorder and science over superstition as universal values with which to defeat the old orders, the old ruling classes . . . with their outmoded ideas. Modernity was revolutionary . . . and was the founding complex of beliefs upon which capitalism as a new mode of production and a transformed social order was established. (1997: 5–6)

The period of modernity is associated with a number of influential developments in scientific practice. First, there is the idea of the importance of reason and the search for rational explanations of human development. Alain Touraine (1995: 9) notes that: 'The idea of modernity makes science, rather than God, central to society and at best relegates religious beliefs to the inner realm of private life.' Alongside this comes the search for the 'laws' governing material and spiritual progress. The notion of a 'deep current of natural progress' was expressed by Kant as follows:

> I will therefore venture to assume that as the human race is continually advancing in civilization and culture as its natural purpose, so it is continually making progress for the better in relation to the moral end of its existence, and

that this progress, although it may be sometimes interrupted, will never be broken off or stopped. (cited in Nisbet, 1969: 117)

In the mid-twentieth century, the approach to ageing as a social and scientific problem was placed squarely within this modernist framework. Longevity was both emblematic of human progress, but a challenge at the same time, one that would require a systematic response from the natural and social sciences. The handbooks edited by Birren and his colleagues were consistent, as Thomas Cole (1992) suggests, with the Enlightenment vision of progress achieved through science and cumulative knowledge. This project, Cole argues, was informed 'by a quest for scientifically-valid explanations of human ageing as a phenomenon dependent, according to James Birren, "on the influence of genetics, physical and social environments, and individual behaviour" ' (Cole et al., 1992: xii).

But the context for this work was central both in shaping the research agenda and in influencing ideas about how people might experience growing old. Old age was rediscovered in a period where despite pessimism about the costs of ageing, there was clear resolve to tackle what was viewed as the new set of challenges confronting modern societies. Crook et al. suggest here that:

> For a period around the middle of the twentieth century . . . it became possible to elaborate a vision of modernity in which a predictable, progressive and fundamentally benign process of 'modernization' would become diffused throughout the world. (1992: 228)

Redefining and reconstructing old age became an important component within this agenda. Growing old was to be moved from its association with the Poor Law, to a new identity built around the rights of citizenship associated with the institutions of the welfare state (a theme identified by T.H. Marshall (1949) in his study *Citizenship and Social Class*). The institutions of modernity thus contributed to a specific discourse and praxis in determining the images and relationships associated with ageing. The most important of these may be summarized in respect of three institutional sectors: first, the development of biomedicine; second, mandatory retirement; third, the welfare state. These three areas provided both a set of responses to the needs of elderly people, and also a vision of a different future for growing old. The elaboration of this provided the basis for the social construction of old age in the mid-twentieth century. Equally, the unravelling of some of the key institutions associated with it, has created deep uncertainty about the future of ageing as we move into the twenty-first century. Before exploring the latter in Part II, we shall first summarize the main components of the reconstruction of old age over the past 50 years.

The rise of biomedicine

The first point to note is that interest in gerontology emerged alongside what was to be a dramatic expansion and institutionalization (in the USA especially) of the natural sciences. Achenbaum makes this point as follows:

> Gerontology emerged as a field of enquiry in an era of Big Science. As the scale of the scientific enterprise increased, researchers on ageing defined and organised their work to take advantage of new opportunities. Investigations were undertaken by multidisciplinary teams working in translaboratory networks. Borders between science and technology, and between basic and applied research [were to grow] fuzzy, sometimes irrelevant. (1995: 121)

Achenbaum goes on to suggest that gerontology emerged as a field of enquiry at a time in which the USA was, as he puts it, 'awestruck' by the power of science to facilitate material progress. Science – and especially the biomedical sciences – was seen as the medium for tackling many of the problems and challenges associated with ageing (see also Katz, 1996). This itself met with considerable support from certain groups of older people. Elderly people, the middle classes especially, were beginning to challenge the fatalism which had traditionally surrounded old age. With the rise in membership of occupational pension schemes, the attraction of a healthier old age became clear (Burns and Phillipson, 1986). At the same time, belief in the power of medicine and doctors in particular, also began to grow during this period (Porter, 1984).

These developments led to a number of important characteristics relating to the way in which old age developed from the mid-twentieth century. First, there was what Estes and Binney (1989) were to describe as the 'biomedicalization of ageing', this having two central features: '(1) the social construction of ageing as a medical problem (thinking of ageing as a medical problem), and (2) the praxis (or practice) of ageing as a medical problem' (Estes and Binney, 1989: 587). The approach adopted by the biomedical model was to view the ageing process as characterized by various processes of decline and decay. Estes (1993) summarized this perspective as one that saw old age as a medical problem that could be alleviated, if not eradicated, through the 'magic bullets' of medical science. The focus was on individual organic pathology and medical interventions, with physicians placed in charge of the definition and treatment of old age as a disease.

A second important feature that followed from this concerned the crucial role of the pharmaceutical industry in determining appropriate responses to the 'problem' of old age. In the post-war era, effective medicines multiplied at an unparalleled rate in countries such as the USA and the UK (Lipton and Lee, 1988; Midland Bank, 1985). Inside the National Health Service, for example, proprietary drugs grew in importance: from around one-fifth of all prescriptions in 1950, to nearly half just seven years later. The yearly NHS drugs bill grew at an increasingly faster rate, approaching £2,000 million by the mid-1980s. Underpinning the drugs boom was the demand for tranquillizers (from the mid-1960s onwards), anti-hypertensives (from the mid to late 1960s), and non-steroidal anti-inflammatory drugs (NSAIDs) (from the mid-1970s). By the 1970s, in the UK, one in five of all elderly people was taking three or more medicines daily; one in ten was taking four or more.

The drug companies undoubtedly flourished given the market provided by an expanding elderly population. Some of this expansion reflects the greater prevalence of disabling conditions that accompanies an elderly population. However, it is possible to trace other factors that contributed to this growth. First, drugs emerged as the treatment of 'first choice' partly through the absence of alternatives. There was, for example, very limited awareness of the role of preventive medicine (perhaps even less than in the inter-war period), and doctors were given little encouragement to think beyond what the drug companies might be offering.

Second, drugs increased in importance to older people in part because the danger regarding their use was (and continues to be) underplayed. General practitioners, especially in the 1950s and 1960s, relied upon the drug companies for information about new medication. There is some evidence that this information was used rather more in conditions affecting older people; in other areas, the doctor relied upon his/her own training or neutral sources (Burns and Phillipson, 1986). Unfortunately, the drug companies almost certainly underestimated (or in many cases denied) the harmful effects of drugs on elderly people.

Third, the very lack of facilities and resources was (and continues to be) a factor promoting drug use. Moreover, the policy of community care (which began to be developed in the UK from the 1960s onwards), although attractive to those anxious to stimulate a move away from care in long-stay settings, actually created new problems, given the failure to control and audit the prescribing of drugs. The end results were the numerous stories of 'drug hoarding' and abuse of repeat prescriptions, which unfolded in the 1970s and 1980s (Tuft, 1982). Almost invariably it was older people who were cited in these stories. But the message – that professionals were themselves responsible for the problem and that drug companies had the most to gain – was usually ignored.

The dominance of biomedicine was, however, a crucial element in the discourse about ageing. Older people learnt to interpret their problems and anxieties increasingly through the medium of doctors in general, and drugs in particular (reflected in the dramatic expansion in the use of psychotropic drugs). As a result of this, the biomedical revolution in the mid-twentieth century held out the promise that the infirmities of old age could be held at bay – suspended at least until the 'fourth' as opposed to what Laslett (1989) and others were to describe as 'the third age'.

This belief was to be assisted by the second important pathway through which old age was constructed in this period – namely that concerning the emergence and institutionalization of retirement.

The triumph of retirement

If the biomedical revolution held out the promise of a healthier old age, retirement was to develop as an institution that provided a framework for developing the broad field of social and leisure activities. Graebner (1980), in his book *A History of Retirement*, sees the post-war years in the USA as a period in which retirement triumphed over alternative methods of dealing with the aged (see also Calhoun, 1978). In the USA, this reflected the steady growth in pension plans, and the extension of social security to additional groups within the workforce. However, a contributory factor was the 'aggressive marketing' of retirement, as part of an attempt to provide a meaningful substitute to work for older people.

The growth of a retirement industry (books, educational films, retirement communities) can be clearly identified in the USA from the late 1940s. Retirement preparation was one element of this, with a number of US universities in the early 1950s starting to offer information and advisory programmes for retirees (Phillipson, 1981). This development was subsequently taken up by industrial corporations as well as trade unions such as the Union of Automobile Workers (UAW). A survey by Tuckman and Lorge (1952) in the early 1950s, of 113 of the largest organizations in the USA, found that around 40 per cent were claiming to have some kind of pre-retirement programme already in operation. Subsequent research was to confirm this growth in interest, although optimism was tempered by the limited scope of many of the programmes implemented (Wermel and Beidemann, 1961; Siegel and Rives, 1978).

Although the immediate post-war period in Britain and the USA, raised the possibility of older people being encouraged to defer retirement for as long as possible, the reality was that governments in both countries began to redefine old age as a period to be spent outside of the workplace (Phillipson, 1982; Graebner, 1980; see also Chapter 5). In the case of Britain, by the late 1950s there was general appreciation that trends in the labour force were making permanent retirement at 60 or 65 increasingly likely. This was the central argument, for example, of the pioneering work of Ferdinand Le Gros Clark. His study *Work, Age and Leisure* was published in 1966, and had as its subtitle: *Causes and Consequences of the Shortened Working Life*. Clark's was a prophetic study which looked ahead to the emergence of groups of older people existing outside the labour market, with independent lifestyles and values and expectations of their own. This issue had also been explored in an influential collection of papers edited by Robert Kleemeier (1961), entitled *Aging and Leisure: A Research Perspective into the Meaningful Use of Time*. Kleemeier set out the underlying framework for the volume in the following way:

> While the shortening of the work week is probably the prime stimulant to the evident increase in leisure; decreasing employment among older workers is a generally ignored but, nevertheless, major contributor to the total amount of free time available to the adult population. Industry tends to view with suspicion the productive capacities of older workers, particularly when younger and seemingly more efficient persons are available to man its plants. The existence of a governmental social security scheme along with private pension programs presumably takes the sting out of retirement, and from management's point of view makes it a desirable alternative to attempts to provide suitable jobs for those eligible for retirement. The net result of these two factors is the large-scale retirement of older workers with vast increases in the amount of free time available to them. (1961: 5)

In the USA, it was precisely this development that led to what Graebner terms as 'the selling of retirement'. He describes the process as follows:

> Life insurance companies, deeply involved in the pension business, were the leading purveyors of the message that retirement, far from being evidence of maladjustment, was a bounty bestowed by the society and by the pension. Like any other normal period in one's life, it required careful preparation on the part of the individual and his employer . . . Speaking at a 1952 session of the National Conference Board, [a] Mutual Life Assurance Company vice-president . . . suggested preparing employees for retirement beginning at fifty. 'Just recently', he said, 'house organs that are coming to my desk have been doing a splendid job of selling the idea . . . and the fact that old age can be beautiful and that the best of life is yet to come . . . That is done by constant stories of happily retired people telling what they do, but still more of course emphasizing what they did to get ready for the life they are now living.' Retirement, as the life insurance agents emphasized in advertisements published in over three hundred newspapers in the late 1940s, was the joy of being at the ball park on a weekday afternoon. (1980: 231)

In the case of Britain, retirement took longer to realize its potential. Although retirement manuals started to be published from the early 1950s (see, for example, Chisholm, 1954), initial attention was directed at the social and psychological problems created by compulsory retirement.

The connection between retirement and poor health was explored in numerous medical studies in the 1950s.[2] The sociological studies were fewer, but followed the same theme in equating retirement with a deterioration in mental well-being (see, for example, Townsend, 1955; Tunstall, 1966).

However, by the late 1950s and early 1960s research, such as that by Emerson (1959), was beginning to suggest a more optimistic view; while confirming that retirement had some initial impact in increasing anxiety, Emerson noted that problems tended to be resolved after a period of transition. Moreover, his research suggested that even during the first year of leaving work, retirement itself had little effect on physical or mental health. The findings in Richardson's study of 244 men come to a similar conclusion:

> The extremes of complete contentment and bitter dissatisfaction with retirement were easily discerned but the majority of statements revealed mixed feelings; attitude to retirement was the product of a number variables – state of health, the meaning of former jobs, length of retirement, use made of retirement, the relationship with family and wider social groups – all of these in varying degrees and diverse ways affected the replies. (1956: 385)

In general terms, however, the 1950s was important in confirming a policy, first established in the inter-war period, that older workers had both less need, as well as less of a right to paid work. On the former, Rowntree (1947), in his report on old people, suggested that real poverty in old age had been virtually eliminated; a view which was to go largely unchallenged until the publication in 1965 of Townsend and Wedderburn's *The Aged in the Welfare State*. On the latter, there was a hardening of the view – between both trade unions and employers – that older workers should, through more generous state and occupational pensions, be allowed to leave the labour force (Hannah, 1986). Both groups saw this as a mechanism for expanding the routes to more senior jobs and for increasing the supply of younger workers. It also reflected a growing belief on the part of employers that older workers were simply less efficient and less productive (Laczko and Phillipson, 1991).

By the end of the 1950s, therefore, retirement was being actively promoted and encouraged as regards its value and benefit for worker and employee alike. The idea of a period of 'active retirement' following the individual's main career, became an important constituent in the reconstruction of the life course. But the idea of the retiree as a 'leisure participant' was also reinforced by another important element, the access of the individual to rights from the welfare state. Here was the basis for the dual identity that shaped old age from the mid-twentieth century onwards: on the one hand, the idea of active retirement; on the other hand, support from the welfare state when independence was threatened. The development of these two aspects brought the promise of

security for older people. The issue of welfare support will now be
briefly reviewed.

The 'triumph' of welfare

Ellis Smith, M.P., told the House of Commons in November 1938: 'Old
grandfathers and grandmothers are afraid to eat too much food lest they
should be taking the bread out of the mouths of their grandchildren'. Another
M.P. told of 'an old man bent and worn, who has worked in the steel industry
all his life', and who had said: 'I only have 10s 0d a week. I am living with my
son, but his wife says she can no longer afford to keep me. I don't know what
to do. I don't want to go to the workhouse, but there is nothing else to be
done'. (cited in Branson and Heinemann, 1971: 229)

I can remember this particular day. Everything was in a radius of a few
minutes' walk, and she [mother] went to the opticians. Obviously she'd got
the prescription from the doctor. She went and she got tested for new glasses.
Then she went further down the road . . . for the chiropodist. She had her feet
done. Then she went back to the doctor's because she'd been having trouble
with her ears and the doctor said . . . he would fix her up with a hearing aid.
And I remember – me mother was a very funny woman – I remember her
saying to the doctor on the way out, 'Well the undertaker's is on the way
home. Everything's going on, I might as well call in there on the way home'.
(Alice Law recalling 5 July 1948 when the Health Service came into being
and the new social security legislation came into force, cited in Hennessy,
1993: 174)

In the mid-twentieth century a significant change occurred in the
history of old age. Hitherto, income in old age had been largely means
tested, with stigmatization and the inevitable loss of status for beneficiaries. After the Second World War, however, growing old became
framed within the context of the new language of 'social rights' and
'social citizenship', these especially being associated with the post-war
reforms in Britain, and the principles of the 1942 Beveridge Report
(Myles, 1996).

The reforms were built around four main elements: first, a comprehensive and universal welfare state based on the idea of shared citizenship; second, the rapid expansion of benefits and entitlements; third, the
maintenance of full employment within a framework of Keynsian
demand-management; fourth, sustained economic growth.[3] Pierson summarizes the expansion in public expenditure which followed on from
this:

. . . in Western Europe in the early 1930s, only about a half of the labour force
was protected by accident, sickness, invalidity and old age insurance. Scarcely

a fifth were insured against unemployment. However, by the mid-1970s, more than 90 per cent of the labour force enjoyed insurance against income loss due to old age, invalidity and sickness; over 80 per cent were covered by accident insurance and 60 per cent had coverage against unemployment. The average annual rate of growth in social security which stood at around 0.9 per cent in 1950–5 had accelerated to 3.4 per cent in the years 1970–4. Broadly defined, social expenditure which had in the early 1950s consumed something between 10 and 20 per cent of GNP had grown to between a quarter and something more than a third of a rapidly enhanced GNP by the mid-1970s. (1991: 128)

What it is important to capture here though is the sense in which the welfare state created not just a mechanism for distributing income and services, but also a distinctive image about elderly people themselves. Older people had come to symbolize all that was wrong about pre-war society. The idea that a particular generation should carry the burden of risk attached to a particular point in the life cycle was now to be challenged. The war itself had demonstrated the way in which the risks of life were experienced by everyone. Goodin and Dryzek (1987) express this point as follows:

Under [wartime] conditions, anyone's future might be your own. That forces each of us to reflect impartially upon the interests of all. Welfare states and such like constitute the appropriate institutional response. These responses get frozen and persist well beyond the moment of uncertainty that gave rise to them . . . Wartime uncertainty and risk-sharing seem to us to provide a particularly powerful explanation . . . of the origins . . . of the post-war welfare state. (1987: 67)

The welfare state created – or set out to create – the basis of a new identity for older people. The idea of sharing the risks attached to growing old was built around the theme of intergenerational solidarity. Society – represented by its constituent generations – was now accepting of the idea of ensuring proper standards of health and well-being in old age (a theme reflected in the 1948 United Nations *Universal Declaration of Human Rights*). Inevitably, achieving this required a significant degree of redistribution between generations: first, because benefits had to be paid ahead of contributions; second, because improvements to programmes were given to current as well as future beneficiaries; third, because of the financing of the system on a 'pay-as-you go basis', with benefits paid out of current revenues (Myles, 1996).

In Britain, the welfare of older people was in essence defined in three main ways for much of the 1950s and 1960s. Pensions were the first and overriding concern, an issue which 'dominated the agenda as much as relief payments had done in an earlier era' (Parker, 1990: 8). Next was the focus on residential and institutional care (a feature of the 1948 National Assistance Act). Then there was the role of the voluntary sector (under the aegis of bodies such as the National Old People's Welfare Council), in providing a limited range of domiciliary provision within the community (Roberts, 1970).

Of continued importance, however, was the role of the family in providing essential support to frail older people (illustrated in studies such as those by Sheldon (1948), Townsend (1957), and many others). In this context, the post-war period created one welfare state for the old (largely built around retirement pensions and residential care), but kept in place the existing 'welfare state' built around the families of older people. These two 'pillars', along with support from the voluntary sector, represented the form in which old age was constructed as a welfare issue and problem.

It is not the purpose of this book to debate the advantages and disadvantages of this type of arrangement. Much research has already focused on the latter, notably in respect of the 'social creation of dependency' (Walker, 1980), the undue emphasis on residential care (Means, 1986), and the limited provision for care in the community (Parker, 1990). Of greater interest here is the argument that for all its limitations, the welfare state did seem to provide a sense (albeit a limited one for many older people) of a different kind of old age than had gone before. Hennessy's respondent cited at the beginning of this section may have embroidered her story somewhat, but the point is clear: first, that the welfare state seemed to be offering some answers to the range of problems that do affect many people at some point in old age; second, that it had begun to erase at least some of the chronic fears attached to growing old.

Conclusion: the modernization of ageing

On this last point, even if the early experience of the welfare state seemed, for the old, to be hugely disappointing, it still appeared to be offering an advance on what had gone before. Moreover, taken alongside the gradual acceptance of retirement, there was the sense of a more stable end to the life course than had previously been the case. In fact, what was on offer may now be seen as limited to a relatively short time span (20 years at most). This period (roughly from 1950 to 1970), represents the high point of the 'modernization of ageing'. Old age was dragged into the modern world through a combination of biomedicine, mandatory retirement, and the growth of the welfare state. But as a framework for the social construction of old age, fundamental problems were soon to appear. On the one hand, biomedicine continued as an element influencing the way in which problems and issues associated with ageing were viewed. On other hand, the institutional pathways through which old age was constructed – notably those associated with retirement and the welfare state – began to be transformed from the 1970s onwards. In the next chapter, we discuss the wider context for these changes, before going on to review some specific examples in Part II.

Notes

1 See Grimley-Evans (1997) for a summary of the history of geriatric medicine.

2 The literature on the impact of retirement is summarized in Phillipson (1993).

3 Lowe (1993) provides an excellent critical review of the development of the welfare state.

4

GROWING OLD IN A POSTMODERN WORLD

During the 1960s, a new type of old age started to unfold. Elderly people (led by charismatic figures in the USA such as Maggie Kuhn) began to demand a stronger presence within political and social institutions (Kuhn, 1991). The idea of the 'third age' of activity and leisure was born; older people became 'senior citizens' in societies that had grown comfortable – notwithstanding the burst of generational warfare in the 1960s – with ideas of solidarity and exchange. Running alongside this, however, had also come a radical change to the environment facing older people. Retirement and the welfare state had developed (along with biomedicine) as two of the 'big ideas' of modernity. They formed part of the development of the modern life course, with individuals constructing their lives around what Best (1980) was to describe as the 'three boxes' of education, work and leisure.[1] Thomas Cole summarizes the historical development of this process as follows:

> Set free from older bonds of status, family, and locality, middle class individuals increasingly came to view their lives as careers – as sequences of expected positions in school, at work, and in retirement. Since the nineteenth century, this pattern of expectations has become both statistically and ideologically normative, constituting what Martin Kohli aptly calls a 'moral economy of the life course'. By the third quarter of the twentieth century, Western democracies had institutionalised this 'moral economy' by providing age-homogenous schools for youthful preparation, jobs organized according to skills, experience, and seniority for middle-aged productivity, and publicly-funded retirement benefits for the aged who were considered too slow, too frail, or two old-fashioned to be productive. (1992: 240)

This vision of a stable life course started to unravel during the 1970s, with the assault coming from a variety of directions. First, western economies – increasingly from the mid-1960s – were unable to maintain the policy goal of full employment. The numbers of people facing long-term unemployment and premature retirement grew rapidly, this resulting in a destabilization of the institution of retirement (see Chapter 5).

Second, the generational accord that had underpinned the welfare state in general, and the 'retirement wage' in particular, was increasingly questioned. During the 1970s notions of generational equity began to surface, with complaints that older people were achieving levels of prosperity and welfare security unlikely to be attained by their children. Instead of workers being seen as future pensioners (in the language of generational exchange), the debate was framed in terms of 'workers versus pensioners';[2] the increase in the number of old people being blamed for ills such as excessive social expenditures and economic inefficiency.

Finally, the structure of the modern life course was itself the subject of critical attack. Increasingly, it was viewed as contributing to the alienation and malaise experienced by older people. Thomas Cole (writing from the perspective of humanistic gerontology) defined the problem in the following terms:

> The ideal of a society legitimately ordered by the divisions of a human lifetime is now under siege in large part because its view of old age is neither socially nor spiritually adequate and because the social meanings of life's stages are in great flux. Recent critiques of ageing in the modern life course have also reflected a dawning awareness that ageing is much more than a problem to be solved. In some quarters, it is becoming clear that accumulating health and wealth through the rationalized control of the body is an impoverished vision of what it means to live a life. In 1964, Erik Erikson noted that 'as our world-image is a one-way street to never ending progress . . . our lives are to be one-way streets to success – and sudden oblivion'. (1992: 241)

This emergent crisis about the meaning of old age chimed in with a wider discourse about the changes set in train by the transition from a modern to a postmodern world (Conrad, 1992). This development is clearly reflected in the transformation of institutions such as retirement and the welfare state. But they indicate also (as Cole, for example, suggests) a more profound transformation in the western experience of growing old. To assess some of the factors that have influenced this change, the focus of this chapter is on the new set of circumstances and conditions brought about by the characteristics of what are termed 'postmodern societies'. We shall also focus on the changes these have brought for the identity of older people, exploring some of the tensions and ambiguities generated by the experience of social change.

Social change in the period of late modernity

The argument of this chapter is that changes to the institutions of retirement and the welfare state are bound up with what Giddens (1991)

defines as a period of 'late modernity', or what has been more generally
termed as the move towards a postmodern society (Bauman, 1992;
Kumar, 1995). Despite the different points of emphasis between these
terms, areas of agreement are also apparent. First, significant changes are
identified within industry, with flexible forms of work organization
increasingly displacing mass production (broadly conceived as the shift
from an industrial to a post-industrial society). Second, the globalization
of social life, with ties of interdependence affecting all communities and
countries of the world. Third, a weakening in the institutions and
practices of the nation state. In relation to this last point, Kumar observes
that:

> Mass political parties give way to the 'new social movements' based on
> gender, race, locality, sexuality. The 'collective identities' of class and shared
> work experiences dissolve into more pluralized and privatized forms of
> identity. The idea of a national culture and national identity is assailed in the
> name of 'minority' cultures – the cultures of particular ethnic groups, religious
> faiths, and communities based on age, gender or sexuality. Post-modernism
> proclaims multi-cultural and multi-ethnic societies. It promotes the 'politics of
> difference'. Identity is not unitary or essential, it is fluid and shifting, fed by
> multiple sources and taking multiple forms . . . (1995: 122)

The issue of identity is fundamental to much of the literature about
postmodern society. Anthony Giddens (1991), in his book *Modernity and
Self-Identity*, is concerned with the emergence of what he sees as new
mechanisms of self-identity, these both shaping and being shaped by the
institutions of modernity. In a late modern age, self-identity becomes a
'reflexively organised endeavour'. Giddens presents a picture of the self
as a 'reflexive project', built around the development of 'coherent, yet
continuously revised, biographical narratives'. Furthermore, these are
seen to operate on the basis of choice and flexibility, this replacing the
rigidity of the traditional life cycle with its predetermined rites of
passage.

The idea of reflexivity is also central to the work of Ulrich Beck (1992),
as developed in his book *Risk Society*. Here, Beck presents a dystopian
view of a rampant industrialism, generating risks and hazards on a scale
surpassing all other historical periods. Such risks – illustrated by the
threat of toxins and pollutants on the environment – exert a global reach,
albeit affecting some communities and social groups more than others.
For Beck, challenging such threats will only be achieved at the point
when society becomes truly reflexive – the period of reflexive modernization. This may be conceived in terms of individuals and the lay public
exerting control and influence on the shape and character of modernity.
Reflexive modernity thus challenges the insecurities introduced by the
process of modernization. At the core of the theory is the thesis that: '. . .
the more societies are modernised, the more agents (subjects) acquire the

ability to reflect on the social conditions of their existence and to change them in that way' (Beck, 1992: 10).

Beck's approach is based upon a three-stage periodization of social change, comprising: first, pre-modernity; second, simple modernity; third, reflexive modernity. Scott Lash notes that with this model simple modern societies are not yet fully modern. He argues:

> In this context reflexive modernity comes after simple modernity. Put another way, traditional society here corresponds to Gemeinschaft; simple modernity to Gesellschaft; and its successor to a Gesellschaft that has become fully reflexive. The motor of social change in this process is individualization. In this context Gesellschaft or simple modernity is modern in the sense that individualization has largely broken down the old traditional structures – extended family, church, village community – of the Gemeinschaft. Yet it is not fully modern because the individualization process has only gone part way and a new set of gesellschaftlisch structures – trade unions, welfare state, government bureaucracy, formalised Taylorist shopfloor rules, class itself as a structure – has taken the place of traditional structures. Full modernisation takes place only when further individualization also sets agency free from even these (simply) modern social structures. (1994: 114)

The implication of this argument, then, is that reflexive modernization involves a separation of individuals from the collective structures which had formed in the period of simple modernity. This arises through such factors according to Lash as the crisis in the nuclear family, changes in the influence of class structures, de-industrialization, ecological concerns, and the critique of institutionalized science.

These developments raise important issues for those institutions around which old age was constructed. Robert Atchley (1993), for example, notes that current retirement policies were built around a society based on mass production and mass institutions. The changes affecting both these elements raise important questions for self-identity and social relationships after the cessation of work. More broadly, the implication is that changes to modernity are producing a different type of ageing, and with this a different type (or more accurately types) of identity in older age. The nature of these developments will be now analysed, with a particular focus on the implications for debates within critical gerontology.

Old age and the move from organized capitalism

The model outlined in the preceding section suggests some useful pointers to changes in the social and economic base of the experience of old age. Taking the period of simple modernity, we can see this associated with a specific kind of retirement and old age, this formed within the context of full employment and expanding welfare states. The emergence of retirement coincided in fact with the period known as 'organized capitalism', with the development of mass production along Fordist and Taylorist lines (Laczko and Phillipson, 1991). The latter provided the foundation for the spread of retirement, notably through age-based discrimination within industry, as well as the growth of occupational pensions.

From the 1970s onwards, however, we have entered a period which Lash and Urry (1987) identify as the 'end of organised capitalism', this reversing some of the features identified above. Flexible forms of work and manufacture are accompanied by contraction and fragmentation of the working class. A service class emerges (built around the employment of women and other social groups) which itself contributes to the fracturing of class-based identities. Industrial deconcentration is accompanied by spatial deconcentration, as people and work move out of the older industrial cities. These developments reflect a heightened degree of instability running through capitalist social relations:

> The world of 'disorganized capitalism' is one in which the 'fixed, fast-frozen relations' of organized capitalist relations have been swept away. Societies are being transformed from above, from below, and from within. All that is solid about organized capitalism, class, industry, cities, collectivity, nation state, even the world, melts into air. (Lash and Urry, cited in Kumar, 1995: 49)

Living in a period of 'late modernity' or 'postmodernity' is, then, about experiencing a world where traditional routines and institutions are abandoned. We live instead in what has been termed a 'post-traditional' society, one in which people are charged with the task of negotiating new lifestyles and making new choices about how to conduct their lives (an issue explored by Giddens in his book *Modernity and Self-Identity*).

These changes affect all individuals – no one, as Beck and others would argue – can escape their global reach and consequences. But people clearly differ in respect of how they respond to a world where traditional institutions are pulled apart, and where day-to-day interaction is governed by a greater degree of openness as well as uncertainty. For older people, the implication of some of these changes may be highly positive. Featherstone and Hepworth (1989), for example, analyse what they describe as the 'modernisation of ageing', this involving a distancing from the period of 'deep old age'. They see this process as involving three important characteristics: first, the development of new, more youthful images of retirement, these providing a challenge to conventional models of ageing. Second, what they describe as 'the social construction of middle age', this becoming more fluidly defined as 'mid-life', or 'the middle years'. Finally, there is the development of the contemporary period of extended mid-life into a complex of states of 'being', 'development', and personal growth mediated by *transitional* states or crises. Featherstone and Hepworth conclude that: 'this elaboration of mid-life increasingly implies a flexible, individualised, biographical approach which takes into account human diversity' (1989: 154).

The argument here, then, is that new forms of ageing may generate more positive social images of older people, these helping to displace existing, and somewhat negative, stereotypes. However, as Featherstone and Hepworth admit (see also Bradley, 1996), it may only be the elite and the wealthy who are normally in a position to transgress existing conventions about age or who can afford expensive forms of body maintenance. On the contrary, for most older people, the negative features of ageing may actually increase as, in the period of 'disorganized capitalism', what had been relative secure institutions are broken up and abandoned.

Old age and the search for identity

Despite some of the positive aspects associated with the changes to modernity, it is the insecurities which these entail which concern us here. The argument being put forward is that we have reached a new crisis in the way in which old age is positioned and experienced within the life course. The steady growth in the proportion of older people in the population was, up until the beginning of the 1980s, contained with the dual institutions of retirement and the welfare state. These created a social, economic and moral space within which growing numbers of people could be channelled. Despite initial resistance (as illustrated by the early post-war literature on attitudes to retirement), the basic arrangement came to be accepted: namely, the idea of a period of active retirement, followed by entry into a period of late old age surrounded by a benign welfare state.

In respect of a cultural history of ageing, this could be said to resolve what remained as an area of ambiguity within society – namely that while more older people could be seen as a sign of a mature and prosperous society, 'too many' older people could also be seen as a burden ('passengers' rather than 'crew' as Robert Ensor put it in 1950). For a period of at least 20 years, moving older people into the zone of retirement and the welfare state, buttressed as well by the idea of intergenerational support, held at bay the underlying issue of finding a place and identity for older people. In this sense, economics came to the rescue of demographics in the 1950s. The prevailing view, after the flurry of concern around the Royal Commission of Population in 1949 and the

Phillips Committee in 1954, was that the problems of older people had been largely resolved – notably in relation to pensions and health. True, the issue of loneliness was discussed in numerous research reports, most notably by Townsend in the 1950s and Tunstall in the 1960s, but the assumption was that these problems could be ameliorated by reforms to the relationships surrounding work, retirement and the welfare state. Certainly, the fixed point of discussion was that the meaning of old age was to be constructed out of the evolving institution of retirement on the one side, and the mature welfare state on the other: the family providing an essential link between the two.

The unravelling of these arrangements (explored in Part II of this book) has exposed once again the cultural uncertainties which surround old age. Society is beset, as it was in the 1930s and 1940s (Phillipson, 1982), with anxieties about the most appropriate way to respond to an ageing population. But these uncertainties are given a particular quality by the pressures and insecurities associated with a postmodern age. Arguably, older people have been the group with the most to lose with the breakup of the relationships associated with 'organized capitalism'. For them, the extension of individualization poses a significant threat to identity itself. As Biggs (1993) notes, modern life raises at least two possibilities: the promise of a multiplicity of identities on the one side, and the danger of psychological disintegration on the other. Biggs suggests that in response to these circumstances, individual actors will attempt to find socially constructed spaces that lend some form of predictability to everyday relationships. Yet, in a postmodern world such spaces may be increasingly difficult to locate. This point has been powerfully made by Zigmunt Bauman in his book *Postmodernity and its Discontents*. He argues here:

> In our postmodern times . . . the boundaries which tend to be simultaneously most strongly desired and most acutely missed are those of a rightful and secure place in society, of a space unquestionably one's own, where one can plan one's life with the minimum of interference, play one's role in a game in which the rules do not change overnight and without notice, and reasonably hope for the better . . . It is the widespread characteristic of men and women in our type of society that they live perpetually with the 'identity problem' unresolved. They suffer, one might say, from a chronic absence of resources with which they could build a truly solid and lasting identity, anchor it and stop it from drifting. (1996: 26)

In the case of older people, 'identity problems' have always been a significant issue in societies where issues relating to production and reproduction have traditionally been central both to the social order and to the individual's identity within it. Leonard (1984) makes the point that

ideological discourse is directed, from childhood onwards, to the performance of productive and reproductive roles which gendered class
subjects are expected to perform. Leonard concludes that:

> Familial ideology is especially significant in constructing a self which is
> congruent with dominant conceptions of the activities and capacities involved
> in present or future roles: mother, father, breeder, bread-winner, 'attractive
> young woman', 'useful member of society' and others. But what happens to
> those who do not appear to occupy these central roles? What is the effect of
> [the experience] of marginality on personality? (1984: 181)

In fact, as Leonard (1984) went on to describe, there was a significant
literature dealing with the crisis affecting groups such as the working-
class elderly and the unemployed when confronted with the absence of
full-time wage labour. On the other hand, it is equally the case that older
people have not been passive in their response to mandatory retirement. Although theoretical perspectives such as 'structured dependency
theory' (Townsend, 1981) have tended to emphasize a view of older
people as victims, an alternative reading would stress the existence of
social movements among the old in areas such as education, politics and
the voluntary sector. However, it can also be argued that these movements were built around the notion of a traditional welfare state, with
the gradual evolution of retirement (after a lifetime of work) within this
framework. The problem of marginality raised by Leonard was thus
resolved by elevating retirement into a status which would equal that
associated with work.

From the 1980s onwards, as we shall describe in more detail in
Chapter 5, the crisis affecting retirement illustrated the way which the
problem of social marginality among the old had been contained rather
than resolved in the post-war period. Moreover, what a postmodern
setting did have to offer – namely the ideal of consumption – seemed
only to further marginalize groups such as the old. Bauman, for example,
writes of the accelerating emancipation of capital from labour: 'instead of
engaging the rest of society in the role of producers, capital tends to
engage them in the role of consumers' (Bauman, 1992: 111). But for the
majority of the old, their engagement with society was increasingly
neither that of producer nor consumer. At the same time, the role of the
old as 'icons' of the welfare state, the one group with an inalienable right
to whatever services were on offer, was also under attack. Younger
generations, it was argued (see Chapter 7), were now challenging the
traditional view of 'interdependence'; increasingly generations were seen
as contestants for a diminishing welfare pie (a logical outcome, it might
be argued, of the individualization of daily life in a postmodern setting).

These developments have not gone unchallenged; they have, however,
confirmed the seriousness of the challenge facing older people. In reality,

in terms of their social position they have moved into a new 'zone of indeterminacy', marginal to both work and welfare. Older people experience the world truly as though they were riding (as Giddens (1991: 28) puts in his description of late moder— a 'juggernaut': 'It is not just that more or less conti— d processes of change occur; rather ch— m either to human expecta- relatively abstract descrip- xperience, but it accurately elderly people placed in

th the following example. in days of being moved d) to a community care ge age of 80 and were e died from bronchial received the patients, ed, commented: 'It is rtality rate to occur in stay hospital to a new 7).

upported by a sub- is equally valid to em of frailty alone – a 24-hour period mething else' that sue raised in much n life, namely, to longer sure of a we live. This is ted. We all want and make sense vever, is that in tity have been ecure sense of e postmodern in the period is that while

patterns of fertility and mortality ageing society, we seem to have undercut a language moral space which can resonate with the rights and needs of older people as a group.

This is a big statement and needs much justification if it is not to seem overly simplistic and facile. To put some flesh on the argument, two responses will be made: first, for the remainder of the chapter we will examine a particular theory of the self and examine the sense in which older people meet its criterion. Then, in the second half of the book, the structural changes which have undermined the position of older people will be examined in more detail. Taken together, both should help indicate some of the pressures and changes affecting older people.

The self in old age

Asking questions about the status of the self in old age remains difficult, given the absence of a strong and clearly defined research tradition in this area. But asking questions about the status of selfhood in late life is fundamental to any understanding of the issues facing older people. To illustrate these, some of the arguments developed in Charles Taylor's (1989) important study *Sources of the Self* will now be discussed, and in particular their relevance in terms of the position of older people. Taylor's concern in his study is to explore the basis of what he terms as the 'modern identity'. Essentially, this involves him tracing 'various strands of our modern notion of what it is to be a human agent, a person, or a self' (Taylor, 1989: 3). A central concern of this book is that the frameworks within which people have been traditionally anchored have been made problematic within the modern world. Philosophical or theological doctrines, at least in the western world, no longer have the binding force on people's consciousness that was once the case. Such doctrines no longer explain the world or 'form the horizon' of the whole society in the modern western world (Taylor, 1989). The consequence of this is the crisis of meaning which we now associate as a fundamental condition of living in a postmodern world. At its most extreme, this crisis of meaning confronts the individual as a condition in which: 'the world loses altogether its spiritual contour, nothing is worth doing, the fear is of a terrifying emptiness, a kind of vertigo, or even a fracturing of our world and body-space' (Taylor, 1989: 18).

Perhaps something of this kind gripped the demented souls described earlier. But the condition itself is viewed as general to man/woman in the western world; a feature of the crisis which is seen to characterize the self in the grip of what some would describe (see Chapter 2) as 'instrumental rationality'. Taylor's essential point is that living without a framework for our lives is an impossibility for the following reasons:

> Frameworks provide the background, explicit or implicit, for our moral judgements, intuitions, or responses . . . To articulate a framework is to explicate what makes sense of our moral responses. That is, when we try to spell out what it is that we presuppose when we judge that a certain form of life is truly worthwhile, or place our dignity in a certain achievement or status,

or define our moral obligations in a certain manner, we find ourselves articulating inter alia what I have been calling here 'frameworks'. (1989: 26)

Taylor goes on to argue:

I want to defend the strong thesis that doing without frameworks is utterly impossible for us; otherwise put, that the horizons within which we live our lives and which make sense of them have to include these qualitative distinctions. Moreover, this is not meant just as a contingently true psychological fact about human beings, which could perhaps turn out one day not to hold for some exceptional individual . . . Rather, the claim is that living within such strongly qualified horizons is constitutive of human agency, that stepping outside these limits would be tantamount to stepping outside what we would recognise as integral, that is, undamaged human personhood. (1989: 27)

From this, Taylor draws out the following conclusion:

Perhaps the best way to see this is to focus on the issue that we usually describe today as the issue of identity. We speak of it in these terms because the question is often spontaneously phrased by people in the form: who am I? But this can't necessarily be answered by giving name and genealogy. What does answer this question for us is an understanding of what is of crucial importance to us. To know who I am is a species of knowing where I stand. My identity is defined by the commitments and identification which provide the frame or horizon within which I try to determine from case to case what is good, or valuable, or what ought to be done, or what I endorse or oppose. In other words, it is the horizon within which I am capable of making a stand. (1989: 27)

For Taylor, a crisis of identity occurs in situations where individuals are uncertain of their position in the world. They lack a framework within which day-to-day living assumes a stable significance; the available options seem to lack meaning and substance. People enter a world where the possibilities before them appear unfixed and undetermined. Taylor concludes that: 'This is a painful and frightening experience' (1989: 28).

Taylor's analysis is an eloquent statement of the existential doubts (and nightmares) which often seem to beset older people. Where do they stand in a world in which priorities and values are constantly open to revision and change? What is the moral and existential space to which they are entitled, in a world where social integration is achieved through the operation of the marketplace? This is not, it should be noted, a rehearsal of an old argument that the problem facing older people is that they lack meaningful roles which tie them to society (a perspective which was influential in sociological thinking about older people in the 1950s and 1960s). Rather, there is a much harder argument here: namely, that modern living undercuts the construction of a viable identity for living in old age. To be sure, the idea of older people as a marginal group is not new, and has been debated within critical gerontology for a number of years. But the argument of this book is that marginality is now being experienced in a new and somewhat distinctive way by older people. Marginality, for much of the post-war period, could, it is argued, be reclaimed through the identities constructed out of an emerging consensus regarding retirement and the welfare state. The collapse of this consensus has exposed once again the vulnerable status of the old. But this vulnerability is not just about the material experience of deprivation, it also reaches into the experience of day-to-day life. People now find themselves exposed to situations where they seem to lack identity: 'Who am I?', has become a difficult question for many to answer. For the seven 'frail' older people in a North London care home, few people could provide any answers – least of all those concerned with actually running the service. But in society as a whole – moving into a new century – the idea of an ageing population seems increasingly to offer dubious benefits. In sacrificing one set of institutions for supporting old age, we have left open their replacement. Part II of this book looks at the deconstruction of old age over the past 20 years. The third part explores some alternatives.

Notes

1 Vincent (1995) brings a life course analysis to the study of inequalities in old age.

2 The title of a controversial study, published in 1989, edited by Johnson et al. See Bengston and Achenbaum (1993) for a more balanced view of the intergenerational debate.

SOCIAL CHANGE AND SOCIAL DIVISIONS

5

THE SOCIAL CONSTRUCTION OF RETIREMENT

The first part of this book reviewed, from a number of theoretical perspectives, some of the key changes influencing the lives of older people. The purpose of Part II of this study is to place these developments within a structural context, with a particular focus on employment and retirement issues, changes to the welfare state, and intergenerational relationships. This chapter examines the first of these areas, focusing on some of the key debates around work and retirement in the period since the Second World War. The chapter outlines post-war trends in the employment of older workers, with a summary of the main themes in the development of retirement. The changes identified are then located within the context of alterations to the life course. Finally, the chapter considers recent policy developments which have begun to change the nature of retirement, and early retirement in particular, during the 1990s.

Older workers and employment

Historians and sociologists have argued that the 'triumph of retirement' only took place in the period following the Second World War (Graebner, 1980; Phillipson, 1982; Freter et al., 1987). In the period from 1950 to 1980, retirement grew in three particular ways: first, in respect of the proportion of people reaching retirement age; second, in respect of the decreasing significance of paid work after retirement; third, as regards the number of people who receive state and occupational pensions. In Britain in 1881, 73 per cent of the male population aged 65 and over were in paid employment; by 1951 this had fallen to 31 per cent; and by 1991 the figure had shrunk to below 10 per cent (Laczko and Phillipson, 1991).

Yet the idea of triumph suggests that retirement was viewed as a positive development both in policy terms and among middle-aged people. Both these suggestions have, however, been challenged in the research literature. In respect of the former, retirement (especially in the 1950s) was initially viewed with some hostility in a climate of post-war austerity and manpower shortages (Phillipson, 1982; Morgan, 1984; Blaikie and MacNicol, 1989). At the same time, and especially in Britain (in part because of economic problems immediately after the war), there was particular emphasis on loss of work representing a 'crisis' for the individual.

In the 1950s, retirement was seen as causing 'problems' less because of its financial implications, and rather more because of its social and psychological impact – for example, the loss of work-based friendships and the reduction in status and self-esteem (see Chapter 3). This perspective was explored in a range of studies undertaken in Britain, the USA and elsewhere, and was supported by perspectives drawn from structural functionalism, the prevailing theoretical orientation within sociological studies.

Reflecting the above, although the economic activity rates of older workers have been falling throughout this century, this was not initially viewed as either a permanent or indeed desirable trend. The Second World War had itself led to an increase in the employment of older workers: by the end of the war, 750,000 pensioners were in work and nearly 300,000 had returned to the labour force after having retired (Brown, 1990). The assumption that economic activity would continue at a high rate among older workers underpinned policy debates during the 1950s. Indeed, even up to the mid-1960s, the then Ministry of Labour was projecting that, based on trends up to 1965, economic activity rates for older men and women would remain stable over the period 1966 to 1981. The expectation was that economic activity rates for men would continue exactly as they were, at 98 per cent for men aged 50–54, 96 per cent for those aged 55–59, and 90 per cent for 60–64-year-olds. A slight dip, from 38 per cent in 1966 to 30.5 per cent in 1981, was envisaged for those aged 65 and over. For women, the rates were seen as holding steady for those not married, at 62 per cent for 55–59-year-olds and 29 per cent for 60–64-year-olds, and increasing for married women, from 39 per cent to 52 per cent and 21 per cent to 26 per cent for the respective age groups (cited in Schuller, 1989).

Table 5.1 *Male economic activity rates in Britain, 1971–2001*

Age	Percentage of each age group economically active										
	Estimates										
	1971	1981	1982	1983	1984	1985	1986	1987	1988	1989	1990
Men											
45–54	95.7	94.9	94.0	93.2	93.0	93.0	92.4	91.5	91.9	92.3	92.1
55–59	93.2	89.7	86.8	84.5	82.6	82.6	81.5	79.8	80.7	80.1	81.3
60–64	83.3	70.1	64.6	60.1	57.3	55.3	53.7	55.1	54.8	54.5	54.3
65–69	30.8	16.6	14.8	13.5	14.0	14.4	13.4	13.1	12.3	14.6	14.4
70 and over	10.9	6.6	5.9	5.3	5.6	5.4	4.9	4.7	5.6	5.7	5.4

Age	Percentage of each age group economically active										
	Estimates					Projections					
	1991	1992	1993	1994	1995	1996	1997	1998	1999	2000	2001
Men											
45–54	91.6	91.7	90.9	90.4	90.0	89.2	89.1	89.0	88.9	88.8	88.7
55–59	80.7	78.3	75.8	76.1	73.9	75.5	76.5	76.5	76.3	76.0	75.6
60–64	54.0	52.8	52.2	51.2	50.2	49.6	49.1	49.2	49.3	49.4	49.4
65–69	15.1	14.7	13.0	14.0	15.1	13.4	12.4	12.7	12.9	13.0	13.0
70 and over	4.9	5.7	4.5	4.2	4.5	4.4	4.4	4.4	4.3	4.3	4.2

Source: Office of National Statistics (1997)

Table 5.2 *Female economic activity rates in Britain, 1971–2001*

Age	Percentage of each age group economically active										
	Estimates										
	1971	1981	1982	1983	1984	1985	1986	1987	1988	1989	1990
Women											
45–54	62.1	68.2	68.1	68.2	69.5	69.5	70.4	70.9	70.7	72.3	72.9
55–59	51.0	53.8	52.3	50.9	51.8	52.1	51.9	53.0	52.8	54.3	55.0
60–64	29.0	23.5	22.0	20.8	21.8	18.9	19.1	19.2	19.9	22.9	22.8
65 and over	6.3	3.7	3.4	3.2	3.1	3.0	2.8	2.7	2.8	3.5	3.4

Age	Percentage of each age group economically active										
	Estimates					Projections					
	1991	1992	1993	1994	1995	1996	1997	1998	1999	2000	2001
Women											
45–54	72.8	74.6	74.9	75.4	75.1	75.8	76.5	77.0	77.5	77.9	78.3
55–59	54.6	54.8	54.7	55.8	56.0	54.7	54.7	54.7	54.8	55.0	55.1
60–64	24.0	23.4	24.8	25.7	25.1	25.3	25.7	26.4	27.0	27.6	28.1
65 and over	3.2	3.7	3.5	3.3	3.2	3.1	3.1	3.1	3.1	3.1	3.1

Source: Office of National Statistics (1997)

These projections were, of course, well wide of the mark – especially in respect of the male workforce. Tables 5.1 and 5.2 examine changes in the position of men and women in the 45–54 age group from the 1970s onwards. The tables confirm the steep fall in economic activity for men aged 60–64, especially in the period from 1971–1985 (a drop of 28 percentage points). The change for men aged 55–59 was also highly significant in this period, showing a decline of nearly 11 percentage points. By the beginning of the 1990s, only around 50 per cent of men aged 60–64 would be counted as economically active.

The trends among older women are more complex to assess because of inadequacies in manpower statistics: in particular, the failure of many women to register as unemployed or the omission of part-time workers (the majority of whom are women) from some labour statistics (Dex and Phillipson, 1986). The official statistics for the 1970s and 1980s indicate a marked decline in the percentage of women aged 60 plus who are defined as economically active. In contrast, the rates for women aged 55–59 fluctuated between 51 per cent and 56 per cent between 1970 and 1995 and for women aged 45–54 there was a gradual rise in economic activity. Although the employment situation for mature women workers appears more stable than is the case for men, this is mainly because the decline in older women's activity rates has been masked by the tendency for each succeeding generation of women to have a higher activity rate than its predecessor. Trinder et al. (1992) note that this effect is brought out in a comparison of the number of 55–59-year-old women in employment in 1984 with that for the same cohorts who were 50–54 in 1979. This shows a drop in employment of 23 per cent.

Taking both men and women, the evidence suggests that the marginalization of older employees gathered pace from the 1970s onwards. A number of factors may be cited to explain this trend: first, the concentration of older workers, in many cases, in contracting industries; second, the operation of particular schemes to promote worker redeployment (for example, the Redundancy Payments Act) or replacement (the Job Release Scheme); third, the pressure of mass unemployment; fourth, changing attitudes among government, business, trade unions and older people themselves, in respect of the older workers' right to employment in relation to other, younger age groups (Bytheway, 1986).

There is some evidence that in the move out of recession around the mid-1980s, there were increased opportunities for individuals either to delay their retirement or to find employment after they had left their main work career (Bone et al., 1992). However, the rise of unemployment (and especially long-term unemployment) in the early 1990s, produced further restrictions on the job opportunities available to older workers.

At the same time, for those who remain in work there has been the emergence of greater flexibility in patterns of employment (Brown, 1990; McGregor and Sproull, 1992). In part, this reflects a marked change over the past 10 years in the nature of the labour market for older workers, with the increasing importance of the self-employed, part-time workers and mature women workers. Across the British labour market as a whole there has been an increase in the proportion of people in 'non-standard' forms of employment (Hewitt, 1993). There has been a striking increase in self-employment, from 9 per cent of the total workforce in 1980 to 15 per cent in 1990. Among older workers the increase has been even more marked (Laczko and Phillipson, 1991).

A higher proportion of the labour force in self-employment implies that more people approaching retirement age will not face retirement at a fixed age. Traditionally, the self-employed are more likely to work beyond state pensionable age: first, because they can adjust their hours of work more easily; second, for financial reasons (they are unlikely to have index-linked pensions). A higher proportion of older workers in part-time work also suggests more flexibility, with more people likely to combine elements of work and retirement.

The transition to retirement

Trends in labour force participation have produced significant changes to the institution of retirement. Retirement (defined in terms of entry into a public old-age pension scheme) and withdrawal or 'exit' from the workforce, no longer coincide for increasing numbers of workers (Kohli and Rein, 1991). Thus it is misleading to view the fall in male participation rates simply as part of a trend towards earlier retirement. Retirement, as it is traditionally defined, is seen to come at a predictable point, accompanied (for most men at least) by a pension provided by the state (Laczko and Phillipson, 1991). In contrast, the retirement which emerged – in many industrialized countries – from the 1970s, did not come at the traditional point in the life course. Moreover, many people, who are generally considered to be retired, do not receive a public pension and may not even consider themselves retired.

These developments reflect the emergence of a new phase in the history of retirement. In general terms we can distinguish between, first, the gradual consolidation of retirement from 1950 through to the mid-1960s; second, the acceleration of early exit and complete cessation of work after the age of 60 or 65 in the period after 1970. It is important to establish the contrast between these periods: in 1951 to 1960 the annualized labour force participation rate for 65–69-year-old men was 50 per cent; for men aged 70-plus the figure was 20 per cent. The equivalent figures for the period between 1971 to 1980 were 24 and 8 per cent, and for 1981 to 1990 were 14 and 5 per cent.

The first period can best be described in terms of a steady consolidation of retirement as a social and economic institution (Phillipson, 1978; Harper and Thane, 1989), with the growth of occupational pension entitlements (Hannah, 1986; Brown, 1990) and the gradual acceptance of retirement as an important stage in the life course (Phillipson, 1990). Sociologically, this period can be identified as one in which retirement is viewed as a largely male phenomenon (and problem), a phase which is still subordinate in length and status to that of paid employment.

The second phase of retirement, from the mid-1960s onwards, is marked by a number of critical changes, these arising from the development of more flexible patterns of work and the emergence of high levels of unemployment. These produced what may be termed the reconstruction of middle and old age, with the identification of a 'third age' in between the period of work (the second age) and the idea of a period of physical and mental decline (the fourth age). A characteristic feature of this new period of life is the ambiguity and flexibility of the boundaries between work at the lower end, and the period of late old age at the upper end of the life course. Both now have complex periods of transition, with the ambiguity of 'work-ending' (Schuller, 1989) in the first period, and the blurring of dependence and independence in the second (Bernard and Meade, 1993).

In the case of the retirement transition, the template of previous generations – long work, short retirement – is being dissolved (Schuller, 1989). For many (mostly male) workers, the predictability of continuous employment is being replaced by insecurity in middle and late working life – an experience shared with the majority of women workers (Itzin and Phillipson, 1993). Older workers increasingly find themselves on the margins of the labour market but with a number of years ahead of them before they reach the comparative safety of retirement. The retirement transition itself has become a period of increasing length and complexity. From the 1970s onwards there was an increase in the range of pre-retirement categories and statuses as well as an increase in the number of people entering these positions (Laczko and Phillipson, 1991).[1] The transition has come to be organized on a much more flexible basis with a number of different pathways (see below) which people follow before they either describe themselves or are defined within the social security system as 'wholly retired' (Kohli et al., 1991). The result of this has been increasing uncertainty as regards the position of older workers, both in their attitudes towards leaving work and in terms of their position within society (Estes, 1991).

Retirement and the life course

The above findings need to be placed within the context of more general changes in relation to the place of work within the life course. An important view which emerged during the 1980s was that the changes in retirement patterns were part of what Martin Kohli (1986) and Anne-Marie Guillemard (1989) termed the 'de-standardization of the life course'. The argument here is that withdrawal from work at earlier ages represents the 'breakup' of the type of retirement which emerged in the 1950s and 1960s. In this period, retirement at 60 or 65-years-old became widely established so that, as Harper and Thane observe: 'By the late 1960s it was accepted that the *normal* period of full-time employment would cease for *most* of the population at these ages' (1989: 59). However, as already indicated, it could be argued that this consolidation was a temporary phenomenon, merely a staging post to a further period of change and reorganization.

Accordingly, Guillemard argues that we have entered a situation where the chronological milestones which once marked the life course are no longer visible and that the time for withdrawal from work is no longer fixed at a predictable point. In this new world, Guillemard says:

> There is less and less of a definite order to the last phase of life. The lifecourse is being deinstutionalized. Along with the abandonment of conventional retirement, we also see the break-up of . . . the threefold model which placed the individual in a foreseeable lifecourse of continuous, consecutive sequences of functions and statuses. As a consequence, an individual's working life now ends in confusion. (1989: 177)

These arguments suggest a new form of crisis in the lives of older people, this reflecting the restructuring of work, along with the challenge to traditional assumptions about the nature of the life course. What seems to have 'come apart' (to use Guillemard's phrase) is the notion of a stable period of retirement, built upon an orderly phase of work and occupation within the life course. Work is itself now much less stable as a social relationship. From a sociological perspective, work has been seen to provide not only income and opportunities for consumption, but a broader structure of individual socialization (Kohli, 1988), as well as access to citizenship (Marshall, 1949). Such a view has always been open to criticism, omitting as it does from consideration groups such as older people, unwaged women and children. However, such an approach has become, as Arber and Ginn (1991) suggest, even less sustainable as paid working life has itself shrunk, with the life course for men and women now being organized in equal measure around work (as paid employment) and non-paid activities (within and beyond the home). Following this, the key issue now is how to face the reality that 'being employed' is not really the normal state of affairs for the majority of people. Offe and Heinze develop this point in their study *Beyond Employment*. They argue:

> The gap between the imagined reality of employment and a steady job and the experienced reality of unemployment, underemployment and precarious or

irregular employment is widening, resulting in a growing contingent of marginalized, discouraged, powerless sections of the population, who are often called the 'new underclass'. But because it is supposedly 'normal' that entitlement to income can only be based on the performance of paid work (or that of family members, or at least on the preparedness to do paid work), the income situation suffers the same vicissitudes as the employment situation, save for a social minimum of public assistance. (1991: 2)

For older people this has produced a more fragmented identity for retirement. There are now 'multiple work-endings' and many different types of pathways into retirement. The diversity of these have been highlighted by researchers as follows:

- forced early retirement (Bytheway, 1986);
- voluntary early retirement pathways (McGoldrick and Cooper, 1989);
- redundancy pathways (Walker, 1989);
- disability/long-term sick pathways (Laczko and Phillipson, 1991);
- informal care pathways (Dalley, 1993);
- unemployment pathways (Laczko and Phillipson, 1991);
- discouraged worker pathways (Laczko, 1987);
- the state retirement pathway (Laczko and Phillipson, 1991).

The complexity of the process of withdrawal from work indicates a significant transformation in the retirement experience itself. In this context, the institution of retirement has moved from a period of relative stability in the 1950s and 1960s (albeit within the context of impoverishment for many retirees), to considerable instability in the 1990s (with enduring poverty for some and affluence for a minority). These changes are raising new challenges for those attempting to construct a secure identity for later life.

Contesting retirement

Over the past 50 years retirement, as has been argued in this chapter, has emerged as a key institution in the lives of older men and women. At the same time, within the broad field of economic and social policy, uncertainties and ambiguities cloud the level of support made available to retirees. In the 1950s, and at least up until the mid-1960s, policy was built around employment continuing to be available at least up until state retirement age (if not beyond). From the late 1960s onwards the debate shifts, with governments encouraging retirement as a part of the need to restructure and rationalize manufacturing industry. Retirement – at least in the 1970s and for much of the 1980s – was viewed as highly desirable, not least given anxieties about the need to control high levels of unemployment. By the 1990s, however, policies had once again gone into reverse. Concern about ageing populations had shifted the debate towards how to stem the flow of older workers out of employment, and remove age barriers in areas such as recruiting and retraining staff (Itzin and Phillipson, 1993; Taylor and Walker, 1993).

In line with the above, governments in most industrialized countries had begun a process of rethinking early retirement policies which had been enacted or encouraged over previous decades. The main character-istics of current reforms are as follows: first, a number of countries have raised the age of retirement. Examples here include Germany – from 60 (women) and 63 (men) to 65 – Austria, Italy and France (by raising the number of contribution years from 37.5 to 40). In some cases, an overall increase in the age has been achieved by raising the retirement age of women to bring it into line with that of men (the UK being one such example).

Second, some countries have taken steps to curtail early retirement. This does not mean necessarily that employees will leave the firm or work later, but that the cost of early retirement is being transferred from the state to the individual and, in some instances, to the enterprise.

Third, reducing the level of benefits has been explored by a number of countries. The UK was actually the first to do so when in 1980 it price-rather than wage-indexed the basic state retirement pension (see Chapter 6). However, other examples of benefit cuts include: France, where since 1993 the level of pension has been based on the 25 as opposed to the 10 best years, and where pensions are also now price-linked as opposed to wage-linked; Portugal, where since 1994 the level of pension has been based on the best 10 of the last 15 years as opposed to the best 5 of the last 10; Finland, where the upper limit on civil service pensions has been reduced from 65 to 60 per cent of earlier income; Denmark, where pensions are now liable to tax.

Fourth, moves towards flexible retirement have also been encouraged, for example in Germany, Austria, Italy, Sweden and Spain. The new calculation rules are, however, designed to promote an extension of the pension contribution period. In Germany, Austria and France, there now exists the option to enter gradual or partial retirement before or after the retirement age.

Not all of the above reforms raise objections in themselves. Clearly, it might be argued that promoting gradual or flexible retirement was a reasonable policy to consider for all countries with ageing populations. The major concern, however, is that the reversal in policies on retirement is introducing new elements of insecurity into the lives of older workers. Only a few years ago, early retirement was being viewed as an entirely predictable and welcome development, a sign that the post-industrial society had now finally arrived. Provided that people had reasonable guarantees in terms of replacement income, an extended period of leisure seemed to have much to commend it. But the basis for securing this was to become the subject of considerable debate. On the one hand, the desirability of retirement came to be questioned in societies going through their regular cycle of 'demographic panic'. On the other hand, the financial basis for retirement, far from being secure after successive reforms of pensions, moved towards a new century in a state of muddle and crisis about how best to finance an ageing population.

By the 1990s, the unravelling of the system of retirement had begun to pose a significant threat to the identities of older persons. Retirement seemed no longer to be central – for increasing numbers of men and women – as a system controlling exit from the workplace. Positive outcomes may of course still be possible. Robert Atchley (1993), for example, has written of the need to develop an emancipatory vision of future employment and retirement systems, and to consider the type of economic and social policies needed to promote effective change. The key question, however, will be: who has control over the institution of retirement? Historically, older workers have rarely been able to control the pace and timing of their own retirement: corporate time has taken priority over individual time (notably for women, for black people, and for those from the working class). Whether a different type of retirement will emerge in the period of late modernity remains to be seen. Retirement can still hold out the promise of emancipation but it needs appropriate resources both in terms of ideas and financial support to make this a reality. At the present time, there seems to be a crisis of confidence in both these vital areas.

Note

1 Disney et al. (1997) confirm this development with data drawn from the Retirement Survey conducted by the Office for National Statistics.

6

FINANCING OLD AGE

The previous chapter set out some key changes in the area of work and retirement, with particular emphasis on the reduced opportunities for paid employment in middle and later life. Western societies, as we have seen, have moved large numbers of older people out of the workplace to help cope with high levels of unemployment. For a period at least, retirement, and early retirement in particular, became a valued social and economic objective. The ideal of promoting a healthy and financially secure retirement became a central theme of government social policy, with renewed interest in issues such as planning and preparation for retirement.

Running alongside this development, however, was another somewhat contradictory policy concern, namely that older people were becoming increasingly costly, and that governments in the twenty-first century would need to rethink the obligations and guarantees which had been made in the past. Increasingly, the perception was to be one of crisis regarding the financing of state or public pensions (World Bank, 1994). Greying populations were associated with actual or potential insolvency, with high levels of early retirement, maturing pension schemes and declining worker–pensioner ratios seeming to represent a daunting economic burden (Department of Social Security, 1997).

At one level, such concerns, as already noted, have been expressed in the language of intergenerational conflict: notably, the view that workers are increasingly resistant to paying taxes for benefits which they themselves are unlikely to receive. This particular theme has been an important element in undermining the security of older people, and is explored in greater detail in Chapter 7. At a more immediate policy level, however, the emphasis has increasingly been on restructuring the welfare state, with pension provision at the cutting edge of proposals to privatize what had hitherto been collective responsibilities. By the 1990s, there seemed to be a virtual political consensus that the 'old' welfare state could no longer be afforded. The pay-as-you-go system of financing

pensions was under attack, with moves towards encouraging greater
personal responsibility in respect of financial security in old age.

Thus along with the unravelling of the institution of retirement, came
a broader attack on the financial arrangements associated with the
welfare state. In this chapter we examine the nature of this attack, with a
particular focus on the issue of pensions for older people.

Poverty and pensions

Public provision for pensions has always been a complex and (as with
the broader issue of retirement) a contested area within social policy
(Achenbaum, 1986). Up until the 1950s, public pension schemes in most
countries tended to be modest, both in the amount of money provided,
and in respect of the groups covered within the working population. In
the majority of cases, provision barely reached a replacement rate of
20 per cent of the average wage; in the UK in 1939 the rate was just
13 per cent (Table 6.1). The level of benefit itself reflected the underlying
goal of public sector schemes: namely, that of providing bare subsistence
and reducing the overall level of poverty (World Bank, 1994).

Judged in relation to this last aim, however, public schemes were
rarely successful. Most of the social surveys conducted in Britain during
the 1920s and 1930s identified old age as one of the major sources of

Table 6.1   *Ratio of average pension to average wage in selected OECD
countries, 1939 and 1980*

Country	1939 (actual)	1980 (synthetic)[1]
Australia	19	n/a
Belgium	14	n/a
Canada	17	34
Denmark	22	29
Germany	19	49
Italy	15	69
Netherlands	13	44
Norway	8	n/a
Sweden	10	68
Switzerland	n/a	37
United Kingdom	13	31
United States	21	44
Average	15.4	45.0

[1] Synthetic replacement rates are simulated percentages of final salary for single workers
with average wages in manufacturing for 1980.

Source: World Bank (1994)

poverty.[1] Stevenson records that the New Survey of London Life and Labour (undertaken in the late 1920s) found that:

> . . . in the East End of London, as in the London area as a whole, poverty was still rife amongst the elderly. As the new survey observed, the pension for a single person was in itself insufficient to place them above the poverty line if they were living alone. The London survey found that in many cases the poverty of the elderly was associated with bad housing conditions. For many the Poor Law Institution with its stigma as the 'workhouse' was the final destination when incapacity and lack of support from relatives prevented them from continuing on their own. (1977: 108)

In the 1930s, Rowntree estimated that in York 33 per cent of old age pensioners were living below his (very stringent) poverty line. Rowntree himself was moved to comment on the lives of these pensioners in the following terms: 'They are, indeed, the poorest people in the city. Of course they *do* get an occasional ounce of tobacco, or glass of beer, but only by suffering a little more from cold and undernourishment. A poor drab ending to a life' (cited in Stevenson, 1977: 81).

By 1931, 63.2 per cent of the population aged 65 and over were receiving old age pensions, with 75.5 per cent of those aged over 70 in receipt. However, a contemporary observer noted that:

> The scale of pension is too low for voluntary retirement except in cases where other resources are available. An income of £1 a week is hardly adequate for a married couple who have no other resources, and even this amount is not received unless the wife is over pensionable age. (Owen, 1935: 81)

The Beveridge Report of 1942 was to set out the basis for post-war reforms to resolve the problem of poverty in old age. Beveridge was to build on the insurance principle established by the National Insurance Act 1911, and the Widows, Orphans and Old Age Contributory Pensions Act 1925, rather than follow the non-contributory route of the Old Age Pensions Act of 1908. This meant, as Walker (1986) argues, that pensions were not regarded as a right but were contingent on the establishment of eligibility through the labour market, or 'work-testing'. Moreover, pensions and other social security benefits were to provide only the minimum subsistence floor specifically in order to encourage additional private welfare provision (Walker, 1986: 200).

Beveridge himself regarded publicly financed pensions as the means by which the emerging welfare state would guarantee a minimum income for all its older citizens. But, as Clarke (1996) argues, the assumption that poverty in old age could be eradicated through a universal state pension had been unrealistic from the start, since the level at which it was set was too low to be adequate in itself, and few people had private sources from which to supplement their income. In consequence, the bulk of pensioners continued to live close to or below the poverty line, and were to be 'rediscovered' in the 1960s as one of the largest groups living in poverty (Cole and Utting, 1962; Townsend and Wedderburn, 1965).

Throughout the post-war period the issue of pensions was dogged by uncertainty. Beveridge had himself issued a warning about the scale of provision, suggesting that: 'it is dangerous to be in any way lavish in old age' until, he suggested, 'adequate provision has been assured for all other vital needs, such as the prevention of disease, and the adequate nutrition of the young'. This mood of caution was to spread through numerous reports and reforms over the next 40 years. Walker and Huby (1989: 21) summarize this as follows:

> As early as 1953 an official committee was set up to 'review the economic and financial *problems* involved in providing for old age, having regard to the prospective increase in the numbers of aged' [emphasis added] and it concluded that 'to provide a subsistence rate for all without regard to need would appear to be an extravagant use of the community's resources'. Similar reasoning in 1959 causes the Conservative government to channel extra resources to the elderly through the national assistance scheme rather than through national insurance provision. Likewise the earnings related scheme introduced in 1961 was designed explicitly to limit the burden on the exchequer by increasing the income from contributions. (1989: 21)

The caution surrounding pension reform was itself reflected in the views of most working people, who took some time to be persuaded that retirement might be an attractive alternative to working. At least up until the 1930s, most workers viewed pension funds as largely a means of providing for widows and orphans after death, rather than a way of supporting their own old age (Stearns, 1977). In the USA, Haber and Gratton (1993) suggest that the very concept of retirement was foreign to many workers. They note that right up to the mid-1950s, older male workers tended to move in and out of the labour force; the abrupt transition from work to retirement that dominates contemporary careers being far less common. In Britain, earnings from work – at least until the 1970s – were a crucial source of additional income in old age: in 1971, for example, nearly one-third of the incomes of men aged 65–69 was derived from paid employment.

At the same time, the possibility of a more secure retirement was increasingly glimpsed (and occasionally experienced) by a minority, given the growing importance of occupational pensions. The percentage of the workforce covered by such pensions rose from 13 per cent in 1936 to 33 per cent in 1956. In the short term, however, this development tended to reinforce views such as those of Titmuss (1955) concerning the emergence of 'two nations in old age': one group reasonably secure in its ownership of an additional pension plus savings; the other recieving only the basic pension, this leaving them dependent on means-tested assistance. Townsend and Wedderburn's (1965) survey was to confirm, however, that a large proportion of pensioners were failing to claim the benefits to which they were entitled. Indeed, the figure (in 1998) of around 900,000 who fail to claim benefits seems to have been a relatively constant number throughout the post-war period.

'The golden age of retirement'

Concerns about the growing divisions in old age, coupled with the impact of reports such as those by Cole and Utting (1962) and Townsend and Wedderburn (1965), generated political pressures that ultimately led the way to the creation of a second tier of pensions – the State Earnings Related Pension Scheme (SERPS) – created by the 1975 Social Security Pensions Act. Arguably, this period from the late 1960s to the late 1970s was one of greater optimism about the future of pensions, with significant benefits at last starting to be felt by larger numbers of retirees. Hannah (1986: 126) goes so far as to suggest that retirement in this period had entered a 'golden age', with a continuing rise in the living standards of older people.

This view may seem an exaggeration (and the differences between men and women are important to emphasize in this and all other periods), but it does reflect characteristics of the way in which older people experienced life in the decades of the 1960s and 1970s. First, as Hannah (1986) himself suggests, having grown up in years of war, unemployment and depression, most people had relatively low expectations – not least about their old age. The reality, however, seemed not quite as bad as many had dreaded. Partly this was to do with more people (though still a minority) drawing occupational pensions: 3.7 million by the end of the 1970s. Partly also it reflected the fact that the state pension actually increased in value during this period (Hills, 1995). In 1974, the level of the state pension was raised by 28 per cent, with an annual updating thereafter linked to the higher of earnings or prices. In fact, Johnson and Falkingham (1992) demonstrate that the relative value of the pension kept pace with average gross male earnings throughout the 1970s. Pensioners improved their position in comparison with manual workers, receiving an amount equivalent to almost 23 per cent of weekly manual earnings in 1983 compared with 21 per cent in 1975. Thereafter, for reasons discussed in more detail below, the relative position of the state pension was to be progressively eroded – notably with the breaking of the indexation with earnings.

In addition, the 1970s seemed a time of promise because of the pension reform introduced by SERPS. Although not without its critics, the legislation did introduce a number of important principles into the pension debate: notably, the formula of using the best 20 years of lifetime earnings for calculating pensions; providing protection for employees who changed jobs; and allowing widows and widowers to inherit the whole of the spouse's additional pension. Although the scheme had few immediate benefits for those entering old age, in the longer term its effects (if it had been allowed to continue as originally conceived) would have been considerable. According to Atkinson:

> There can be little doubt that the SERPS scheme as originally introduced would when mature have gone a long way towards ensuring an adequate minimum income in old age . . . The numbers of pensioners on means-tested assistance would have been reduced to a third, and on more optimistic assumptions very few would have had to resort to assistance. (1994: 11)

A final factor in the idea of the 1960s and 1970s as representing improvements to the lives of old people, came in the form of more aggressive campaigns around the persistence of poverty and hardship in old age. The issue of poverty had indeed largely been forgotten in the 1950s, with an assumption that the Beveridge reforms had erased this problem for the generation now in old age. Despite the importance of studies such as Townsend's (1957) *The Family Life of Old People*, which confirmed the existence of extensive poverty among the working-class elderly, there was no ground swell of action about the problem – least of all among older people themselves (Pratt, 1993). The 1960s were to change all this, with a tide of literature confirming the existence of poverty on a massive scale. *The Poor and the Poorest* by Abel-Smith and Townsend (1965) became, as Clarke (1996: 306) observes, 'a peculiar kind of Christmas best-seller, tapping the seasonal market to raise popular compassion of the problem'. This book was published two years after Harrington's (1963) *The Other America*, which had launched a blistering condemnation of the extent of poverty among the USA's old:

> This is no country for old men. The physical humiliation and the loneliness are real, but to them is added the indignity of living in a society that is obsessed by youth and tries to ignore age. These people are caught . . . in a triple 'chain of causality': they are plagued by ill health; they do not have enough money; and they are socially isolated. Some of them are new entrants to the world of the other America, drifting down from a working life of decent wages to an old age of dependency and social workers. A good many are old and poor because they were young and poor, middle-aged and poor. Taken together, they constitute a section of the culture of poverty with over 8,000,000 inhabitants. (1963: 101–2)

Coates and Silburn (1970) continued the attack in their influential *Poverty: The Forgotten Englishmen*. And Shaw's (1971) *On Our Conscience: The Plight of the Elderly*, was a hard-hitting exposure of poverty and neglect among older people living in Sheffield. These studies, along with critiques such as those by Kincaid (1973) of the broad system of social security and taxation, contributed to the development of an important lobby of organizations and individuals campaigning against poverty (notably Age Concern and Help the Aged in relation to older people). Poverty was now out in the open at least, part of what Jackson (1968) was to term as the 'deep and terrible rhythm' running through working-class life.

But the changes described can now be more properly seen as operating on the cusp of the welfare state. Thereafter, and especially into the 1980s, the optimism begins to unravel: membership of occupational pensions among the employed population actually peaked in 1967 (at 53 per cent), declining to 48 per cent in 1991.[2] SERPS was under threat within seven years of its introduction, and numerous (and major) changes were made in the 1986 Social Security Act and again in the 1995 Pensions Act (Creedy and Disney, 1989; Ginn and Arber, 1995).

Such developments reflected a wider sense of political unease about the funding of pensions. In the 1950s, as Johnson and Falkingham (1992) observe, the move from a fully funded to a pay-as-you-go system slipped through without controversy. Economic growth provided a sense that state support for pensions could be guaranteed, so long as income and expenditure were kept roughly in balance each year. In addition, such support was seen as the proper duty of a mature industrial society – an essential pillar of what Marshall, as noted elsewhere, was to view as the rights of citizenship. The 1970s, however, were to bring the initial questioning of the pay-as-you-go system, as social security now came to be viewed as an obstacle rather than an aid to economic efficiency. Given the level of expenditure on pensions, they were inevitably brought into the front line of the debate about the future of the welfare state (Myles, 1984; 1996).

Finally, poverty continued to grow as a problem – for all generations – but the optimism and energy of the anti-poverty lobby was marginalized and neutralized by Thatcherite social policy in the 1980s. By the 1990s, the policies for supporting people in old age had once again entered a period of confusion and uncertainty. Before reviewing some the some of the issues and concerns, a balance sheet of the financial status of the old will first be drawn.

The incomes of the old

Older people occupy a central place in the debate about the welfare state if only because retirement pensions take the largest slice of social security

Table 6.2 *Average annual real increase in benefit expenditure by client group 1978/79 to 1992/93 (percentages)*

	1978/79 to 1992/93	1978/79 to 1983/84	1983/84 to 1986/87	1986/87 to 1989/90	1989/90 to 1992/93
Elderly	2.45	3.51	2.37	−0.74	4.04
Sick and disabled:					
Short-term sick	−3.82	−8.16	2.02	1.80	−7.48
Long-term sick and disabled	8.17	6.52	8.61	5.48	11.35
Total	6.15	3.10	7.60	4.99	11.14
Family	4.26	6.42	5.06	−1.38	5.69
Unemployed	6.82	20.40	3.22	−20.59	21.83
Widows and others	−2.04	−1.98	−1.22	−6.16	1.30
Of which lone parents	7.38	3.92	8.21	9.21	10.63

Source: Department of Social Security (1993)

expenditure – £32 billion in 1996/97. However, it is also clear from the pattern of growth over the past 15 years that expenditure has grown across all client groups and that older people have in fact lagged behind in respect of average increases in benefits (Table 6.2).

In general terms, income in old age in Britain is built around four sources of income: a basic pension provided by the state together with other social security income; a supplementary pension (for example, SERPS, an occupational pension, a personal pension, or some combination thereof); personal savings; and income from employment. It is the changing balance between these elements, the levels at which income is set, and the rules governing access to different sources of income, which largely determine the living standards of older people.

Table 6.3 shows the contribution of these different sources to the gross incomes of older people and how the composition of total income has changed over time. Table 6.4 provides additional information on the composition of the weekly income of pensioners and the changes between 1979 and 1988. The tables underline the long-term trend of the declining significance of earnings, from 27 per cent in 1951, down to just 8 per cent in 1995. The changing balance between the four types of resources is evident in both tables, with the increasing significance of occupational pensions, together with savings and investments, and the continued importance of state pensions/benefits, albeit within the context of fluctuations in their relative value (see below).

In general terms, while the absolute incomes of older people increased in the 1980s, they lagged behind those of the working population. Within the elderly population income inequalities widened, with a small group of around 200,000–300,000 'Woopies' (well off older people) enjoying relatively high incomes (Falkingham and Victor, 1991). To set against this

Table 6.3   *Sources of pensioners' gross incomes in the UK (percentages)*

	1951	1961	1974	1979	1986	1988	1995
All state sources	42	48	55	61	59	51	51
Occupational pensions	15	16	15	16	20	23	24
Savings and investments	15	15	13	11	14	17	16
Earnings	27	22	17	12	7	8	8

Sources: Derived from Table A3, p. 15, Fiegehen (1986) and written answers from *Hansard*, 17 May 1989, col. 222; *Hansard*, 6 November 1992, cols 463 and 483; and Pension Provision Group (1998)

small number of affluent elderly, however, was the persistence of a much larger number of older people existing on low or very low incomes.

Although older people have declined as a proportion of all income support (IS) claimants, the absolute number has remained fairly stable, dropping from 1.9 million in 1970 to an estimated 1.5 million in 1996. At least another two million elderly people receive means-tested housing benefit or council tax benefit. Dependence on social security varies according to both age and gender. There remains a strong likelihood of people aged 75 or over (most of whom are women) receiving income support: in 1996, one in four (24.6 per cent) were in receipt of IS; among those aged 85 plus, it was around one in three (35.9 per cent). There is also likely to be a substantial level of under-claiming among the very elderly population, so these figures are almost certainly underestimates of the level of poverty among the elderly population.

A further illustration of the low incomes of the majority of pensioners is that in 1996–97, only around one-third (3.0 million) of people aged 65 and over were liable for tax, with only a fraction of these (0.15 million) paying at the higher rate (*Hansard*, 9 January 1996, col. 90). Even more compelling is the fact that in 1995, 60 per cent of single pensioners were dependent upon state benefit for 75 per cent of their income; the figure for pensioner couples was 37 per cent (*Hansard*, 10 February 1997, col. 73).

The increasing variety of sources of income has itself widened income inequality among older people (Pension Provision Group, 1998). This point is illustrated in Tables 6.5 and 6.6, which examine gross income by quintiles for single pensioners and pensioner couples. An important difference concerns the contribution of benefit income. Among couples, for those in the bottom 40 per cent of the income distribution, social security payments comprise three-quarters or more of their total income; for the top 20 per cent benefits comprise just one-fifth. For the latter group, two-thirds (64 per cent) of their income is derived from occupational pensions and investments; this compares with just 11 per cent for the bottom 20 per cent.

Table 6.4 *The average income of pensioner units by source (£ per week, 1988 prices)*

Year	State pension/ benefit	Occupational pension	Savings income	Earnings	Total gross income	Tax/NI	Total net income
1979	53.00	13.90	9.50	10.40	86.80	7.20	79.70
1980	53.80	13.80	10.00	9.90	87.50	6.20	81.30
1981	56.50	15.10	12.00	9.20	92.90	7.70	85.20
1982	58.20	15.50	10.60	7.30	91.50	7.10	84.50
1983	61.20	19.00	14.00	8.30	102.50	9.10	93.30
1984	61.20	18.20	12.70	8.20	100.40	8.10	92.30
1985	60.90	21.00	14.50	6.50	102.90	9.10	93.80
1986	63.10	21.70	15.50	7.50	107.80	9.80	98.00
1987	62.10	24.40	21.90	8.30	116.70	11.90	104.80
1988	60.70	27.70	20.00	9.70	118.10	11.70	106.30
Real increase	14 per cent	99 per cent	110 per cent	−6 per cent	36 per cent	–	34 per cent

Notes
1. Component incomes by source are rounded to the nearest 10p.
2. Components may not sum to totals owing to rounding.
3. Percentage increases are calculated using unrounded figures.
4. A pensioner unit is defined as a single person over state pension age or a couple in which the husband is over state pension age.

Source: Family Expenditure Survey, *Hansard*, 6 November 1992, cols 463–4.

Table 6.5   *Mean gross income and its components by quintile, single pensioners 1994–95 (July 1994 prices) – The pensioners' incomes series 1994–95*

	Bottom	2nd	3rd	4th	Top	Mean
Benefit income	65.40	75.50	87.60	93.60	89.80	82.40
Occupational pensions	3.00	8.10	12.00	25.50	94.50	28.60
Investment income	4.00	5.10	5.50	11.20	84.10	21.90
Earnings	0.20	0.50	0.50	2.30	41.20	8.90
Other income	0.30	0.40	0.60	1.10	2.10	0.90
Gross income	72.90	89.70	106.20	133.80	311.60	142.70
Benefit income as a % of total gross income	90	84	82	70	29	

Source: Hansard Written Answers, 14 February 1997, cols 343–4

Table 6.6   *Mean gross income and its components by quintile, pensioner couples 1994–95 (July 1994 prices) – The pensioners' incomes series 1994–95*

	Bottom	2nd	3rd	4th	Top	Mean
Benefit income	108.80	120.00	126.90	125.00	116.00	119.30
Occupational pensions	8.00	22.60	44.60	89.20	219.00	76.70
Investment income	5.10	9.60	15.00	31.30	128.80	37.90
Earnings	0.60	4.70	5.50	13.20	77.80	20.30
Other income	0.80	0.30	3.10	1.00	3.00	1.60
Gross income	123.30	157.20	195.10	259.70	544.60	255.90
Benefit income as a % of total gross income	88	76	65	48	21	

Notes
1. All figures rounded to the nearest £0.10. Components may not sum to totals due to rounding.
2. Income refers to gross income before housing costs (BHC).
3. The quintiles have been constructed based on the equivalized BHC net income distribution.
4. Pensioner units are defined as single people aged at state pension age or above, or couples in which the man is aged at state pension age or above.

Source: Hansard Written Answers, 14 February 1997, cols 345–6

Single pensioners (the majority of whom are women) have a different profile to that of couples. Here, social security payments comprise 70 per cent or more of the total incomes for all quintiles except for the top 20 per cent. For this group occupational pensions and investments comprise 51 per cent of total income.

Hancock and Weir (1994) have confirmed the growing inequality in pensioner incomes during the 1980s. Using data from the General Household Survey and Family Expenditure Survey, they found that the median or mid-point incomes of the richest one-fifth of pensioners grew by nearly 40 per cent during the 1980s, while those of the poorest increased by only 5 per cent. By the end of the decade, the former enjoyed incomes almost three times larger than those of the latter, compared to two-and-a-half times in 1979. In addition, the after-tax incomes for occupational pensioners moved ahead rapidly in the 1980s in real terms compared with the incomes of non-occupational pensioners. In 1979, there was a 13 per cent difference between their median income levels but by 1989 the gap had grown to 50 per cent. Between 1979 and 1991 net income levels actually fell by 6 per cent, after allowing for inflation, among pensioners with no occupational pension.

This profile confirms the importance of gender and social class differences in determining income in later life. The financial problems facing older women are especially serious. Women (in 1997) retired on average incomes of £138 a week – barely 40 per cent of national average earnings. Women are less likely than men to belong to an occupational pension scheme: in 1991 only 3.9 million women were members, compared with 6.8 million men. Also, their schemes were worth less on average than men's: women aged 65–69 have an average income from occupational pensions of just £22 a week; men receive £67 a week.

In general terms, income differences among older people widened in the 1980s and 1990s as, on the one hand, social security benefits were eroded in value, and, on the other hand, a minority benefited from substantial 'second-tier' pensions and investment income. In fact, the increase at the top end of the pensioner income distribution in the last 20 years has been more than twice that at the bottom end (Pension Provision Group, 1998). The explanation for this has been summarized by Johnson and Falkingham as follows:

> . . . it is clear that differentials in later life with regard to income are strongly correlated with factors acquired during working life. Payments of premiums for higher pensions are clearly related to the income and employment history of the individual. Unemployment, part-time work and early retirement may well preclude the building-up of non-state pension contributions for certain groups, especially women. Thus, it is likely that the continued emphasis on private rather than public provision will result in increasing inequality in income within the older age groups. Although the growth of occupational pensions may lead to the emergence of a highly visible minority of wealthy elderly, this group should not be duly focused upon, obscuring the reality of later life as experienced by the poorer majority of pensioners. It is likely that as we go in to the next century, the 'two nations in old age' first identified by Titmuss in the 1950s – those in receipt of an occupational pension and those without – will continue to endure. (1992: 65–6)

The crisis in pensioner incomes

As was shown in the previous chapter, the 1980s was the decade of early retirement, with large numbers of middle-aged people leaving the labour market. In theory, this should have been a time of increased support for pensioners: insecurity at work being responded to with increased financial security directed at pensioner households. In fact, the reverse has been the case, with the financial situation of older people being affected by long-term trends in four major income-generating areas: first, earnings from employment; second, financial support from other individuals within the household; third, income from the basic state pension; fourth income from a 'second-tier pension'. It is the changes in all four of these areas, over the past 50 years, which has led to a crisis in pensioner incomes, along with growing inequalities within the elderly population.

The change in relation to earnings has already been discussed and is bound up with the growth of retirement in the post-war period, along with continued age discrimination within the workplace (Itzin and Phillipson, 1993). However, it is important to emphasize the seriousness of this development in respect of income opportunities for older people. The possibility of income from employment has, historically, been vital for many older people, especially those without an additional pension or with inadequate savings. For much of the 1950s and early 1960s, older people were positively encouraged to work and to play their part in the rebuilding of the economy. Between 1943 and 1955 around one million people deferred their retirement, receiving as a consequence modest additions to their basic pension and the benefit of another source of income (Phillipson, 1978). By the 1970s, however, extra income from this source was clearly an option only for a minority, with even further inroads being made over succeeding decades. By 1993, earnings contributed to less than 1 per cent of the incomes in the bottom 40 per cent of the pensioner income distribution. In contrast, and somewhat perversely, for the top 20 per cent earnings represented a useful 10 per cent of their income.

The collapse of work has, then, been a key issue for the majority of older people – but for working-class pensioners in particular. Alongside this, however, has come another and less obvious loss of income – namely that from other people within the household. The households of older people have changed considerably over the past 50 years. In the late 1940s and through the 1950s, a significant proportion of older people were – for a variety of reasons – sharing accommodation with children, other relatives, or (less commonly) lodgers. Since the 1960s, however, as the research of Richard Wall (1992) has demonstrated, there has been a significant decline in the proportion of older people living with others.[3] Among a number of factors influencing this decline have been the reduction in the average number of children and their earlier and more frequent marriage or co-habitation, greater geographical mobility, the increase in employment opportunities for women over the last 20 years, and the greater availability of housing.

These developments have, it is suggested by Johnson and Falkingham (1992), led to divergent paths for the incomes of non-pensioner as opposed to pensioner households: for the former, trends such as smaller household size and the growth of dual-earners have increased per capita resources; for the latter, the decline in household size works in the opposite direction, as the bulk of pensioner income is derived from the state and is therefore directly determined by the number of people over pensionable age in the household.

The contribution of members of the family to the incomes of the old is a matter of some historical dispute (Gordon, 1988). However, there seems no doubt that the existence of employed relatives within the home would have been important in lifting the incomes of older people with no other income but the basic retirement pension. This much was confirmed in Cole and Utting's (1962) research in the late 1950s and early 1960s. These researchers identified very substantial numbers of older people living close to the poverty line, with a significant group living on or below it. However, Cole and Utting also commented that:

> If this report does not present a more alarmist picture of the real hardship caused by poverty for the old it is largely because of the help which they receive in one form or another from their family and friends. Large numbers of the old people with incomes at subsistence level manage without National Assistance by keeping house with their children or with other relatives and friends. (1962: 103)

In fact, the period in which this report was published was the start of a clear decline in the proportion of older people 'keeping house' in this way: by the end of the century the proportion of older people sharing a household with a child had dropped to around 13 per cent. Of course, children, as numerous studies have demonstrated, remain crucial in terms of care and support for older people. But in the 1990s there is no evidence that they supply regular amounts of financial help; indeed, what evidence there is suggests help is likely to flow *down* rather than *up* the generational ladder. In general, the movement of relatives out of the home has been a significant factor in limiting the pooling of resources. The maintenance of separate households undoubtedly alters the dynamics of this process, with for low income elders the loss of another regular source of financial help.

Changes to employment and housing arrangements would not on their own have produced a crisis in pensioner incomes. The additional element that did eventually weaken the position of a substantial proportion of pensioners was the erosion of the value of the basic state retirement pension. Again, taking the period since 1950, state benefits (and the basic state pension in particular) have been vital in maintaining the living standards of older people. This much was reported in studies such as that by Cole and Utting (1962), and has been confirmed in numerous reports since (Walker, 1993). A study by Hancock and Weir (1994) found that only 12 per cent of pensioners did not consider that the basic state pension was a significant part of their income (or expressed another way, 88 per cent considered that it was). From another perspective, a survey of attitudes to retirement income found 95 per cent of people believing that the state pension should be at least enough to provide for basic needs; 63 per cent thought it should provide more than enough (Hancock et al., 1995).[4]

The reality of course is now significantly at odds with these aspirations. Since 1980 the pension has been linked to rises in prices rather than earnings, with the consequence that it has steadily reduced in value. The value of the basic pension, relative to average (disposable) income, reached a peak of 46.5 per cent in 1983, but by 1992 was lower than it had been in 1948 (Hills, 1993: 51). By April 1997, the rate for a single pensioner was £62.45 per week, as opposed to the £86.00 it would have been if linked to the higher of earnings or prices. The equivalent figures for pensioner couples were £99.65 as against £137.65 (Hansard, 5 February 1997, col. 638). Hills (1997) notes that by 1997 the pension was worth around 15 per cent of average gross male earnings, lower than at any time since 1971, the earliest date for which this calculation can be made consistently.

The long-term implications of this policy are that the state pension will gradually decline to the extent of representing only a fraction of average earnings. Assuming a growth rate of 1.5 per cent per annum in respect of earnings, there would be a drop from the 14 per cent of average earnings in the mid-1990s, to just 8 per cent by the year 2040. With a growth rate of 2.5 per cent per annum, it would fall to 8 per cent by 2018 (Government Actuary, 1990).

These figures raise additional concerns given changes in the final area to be discussed: that of 'second-tier' pensions. After the passing of the 1975 Social Security Act, all employees have been required to contribute either to SERPS or to a 'contracted out' occupational pension scheme (or, later, a personal pension), which would pay a 'guaranteed minimum pension' (GMP) which should be at least as good as that received through SERPS. Government anxieties about the costs of SERPS, however, have led to radical modifications to the original plan. Following the 1986 Social Security Act, SERPS is now calculated on the average of lifetime earnings (rather than the best 20 years). For those retiring after 2008–9, the pension payable will be based on 20 rather than 25 per cent of these earnings. In addition, only half the accrued pension will be passed on to a surviving spouse. Further savings on SERPS were also introduced under the 1995 Pensions Act. Overall, these changes amount to a massive reduction in support for a policy which was of direct benefit to lower paid workers and to women in particular. The scale of the change can be measured by the fact that if the arrangements of the 1975 legislation had remained in place, spending on SERPS would (at 1994–95 prices) have been running at £41 million by 2030. With the changes introduced in 1986 and 1995, the figure will fall to just £12 million (*Hansard*, 2 May 1996, col. 636).

The above trends are extremely serious both for Britain's current older population, and more specifically those retiring in the future. One response has been to encourage people to take out personal pensions developed by the life insurance industry. Given the withdrawal of the state, with the declining value of the state retirement pension and the cuts to SERPS, personal pensions were seen as the way forward for those without effective cover from an occupational pension. The number of people with a personal pension rose in fact from 3.4 million in 1988 to 5.6 million in 1994/5 (Department of Social Security, 1997). Unfortunately, this expansion was to bring new problems, with the misselling of pensions on a huge scale. In the measured tones of *The Times* newspaper (16 July 1997):

> The life insurance companies saw the handing over of pensions provisions in the private sector as a golden opportunity to deprive the public of £4 billion. Life insurance salesman, earning hundreds of thousands in commission, encouraged miners, nurses and other public-sector workers to leave schemes with guaranteed benefits to take out plans where the charges in some cases meant that none of the policyholders' contributions were invested for up to four years.

It is estimated that between 1988 and 1993, an estimated 1.5 million policies were wrongly sold, with the worst affected being those duped into leaving attractive index-linked pensions for private plans. Years later, thousands were still unaware of the mistake they had made and that they could be missing out on thousands of pounds for their old age. A report by the Office of Fair Trading (OFT) (1997) concluded that many personal pensions were of poor value, with benefits eroded by the high costs of marketing and fund management. The OFT found that up to 30 per cent of a fund could be eaten up in charges over 25 years, with salesmen making inflated claims for the returns from active management of personal pensions to distract attention from high charges.

Members of occupational schemes have also encountered problems. The ease with which Robert Maxwell laundered £400 million from his company's pension scheme illustrates some of the flaws in current regulations. Will Hutton (1996) notes that companies regularly claim any so-called pension fund surpluses as their own. The surplus may have arisen from the rise in value of the assets to which both employer and employee contributed – but the surplus is not passed on to the pension fund or pensioners. Instead, the company makes it the excuse for cutting back on its own pension contributions, so that the purpose of many takeovers is to grab pension funds which have surpluses thus saving on employer's contributions (Hutton, 1996: 202; see also Ward, 1996).

The future of pensions

Resolving the pensions crisis will undoubtedly be the major task for government social policy over the next few years. The declining value of the state pension has underlined the urgency of the issues confronting current and future generations of pensioners. Most people still experience retirement as representing a significant cut in their living standards: 90 per cent of people retire on less than the maximum pension of two-thirds of salary allowed by the Inland Revenue. One in four workers is currently making no extra pension provision whatsoever. Future cohorts of pensioners will of course present different income profiles, and there has clearly been the emergence of a significant group of pensioners (around 15–20 per cent of the total) who can live in a reasonable degree of comfort. But all the evidence suggests that for the remaining 80 per cent (women especially) there is the experience of differing levels of financial insecurity. For some this lasts right through old age, this reflecting lifelong exploitation within the labour market. For others, the crisis may come in advanced old age, when savings prove insufficient to meet the costs of care.

These disparities are unlikely to change with future cohorts of pensioners. Indeed, all the evidence shows a widening of inequalities among the employed with many being unable to get access to occupational or personal pensions (or to pay for these on a regular basis). Older women have been hit especially hard by pension changes over the past decade. Cuts in the value of the state pension and to SERPS have been especially damaging to those on low incomes and with no occupational pension, with women the majority in both these groups. Moreover, the raising of the state pension age for women to 65 (for those born after 1950) is highly regressive. Ginn and Arber (1995: 206) argue that this measure will almost certainly reduce the amount of women's state pension income. They point out that:

> Since only half of women are employed in their late fifties, the change will mean that the majority of women will have to wait for over five years for their state pensions. Among those with no private pension entitlements, the majority of non-married women will be dependent on Income Support, while for married and cohabiting women, most of whom will have been accustomed to

earning an independent income, the change will leave them dependent on their partner for financial support.

Despite these problems, the broad thrust of reform – on the part of both Conservative and Labour governments – is towards reducing the role of the state in providing support for old age. In one of its last major initiatives, the Conservatives proposed the privatization of both the basic pension as well as SERPS. Whitehouse and Wolf commented on the proposals as follows:

> In proposing the privatisation of the basic state pension, the government has broken a taboo. It is now possible to imagine almost complete withdrawal of the British state from direct provisions of pensions – if only after a transition lasting many decades. The proposals are radical and are certain to be controversial. But they are also unquestionably clever . . . Repackaged they could even appeal to a New Labour successor. (1997: 27)

In fact, within weeks of taking office in April 1997 the Labour administration announced a major review of pensions.[5] This was spread over 12 months partly because of genuine uncertainty on the part of the government about the best way forward; but also given the need to prepare the public for the inevitable conclusion, namely, that people would increasingly have to take responsibility for their own pension arrangements. The focus of the review has been on ensuring that more people have a second-tier pension, central to which is the idea of a stakeholder scheme under which the private sector would offer approved, low-cost, flexible arrangements. Essential requirements for such a pension would be greater portability than is presently the case, given the requirement for a 'flexible' workforce; low administration charges; and secure arrangements for indexation in retirement. Another innovation concerns that of a 'citizenship pension' for people caring for children and sick or elderly relatives. This is likely to take the form of a SERPS credit or a government contribution paid into a stakeholder pension on the carer's behalf.

Despite the virtues of many of the proposals for a second-tier pension, failure to tackle the declining value of the basic retirement pension will almost certainly add to the insecurities faced by people in older age. The disaster of personal pensions – 'the greatest financial scandal of the century' (The Times, 16 July 1997) – has reinforced the belief of the public that pensions are too complex to understand (a view highlighted in the report of the Office of Fair Trading). This is unlikely to change with the adoption of stakeholder pensions, with the range of new providers (building societies, employers' bodies and trade unions) likely to vary greatly in the quality of advice given to prospective purchasers.

Conclusion: old age and the retreat of the state

The uncertainty surrounding the provision of pensions is a vital element in the destabilization of old age. Confronted with a less predictable life course, people are now coming to realize that financial arrangements for growing old are also fraught with insecurity.[6] Many turn away and just leave the planning of old age to fate: a survey in the early 1980s, for example, reported nearly 40 per cent of men and 53 per cent of women aged 50 plus giving little or no thought to their future retirement income (Ritchie and Barrowclough, 1983). In the present climate, given the experience of many of those who tried their hand with personal pensions, this would seem perfectly rational behaviour. But rational or otherwise, this raises once again the issue of just what old age and retirement is for. If the hope in the mid-twentieth century was that we could at last banish the fear of poverty in old age, 50 years on that still seems to be extraordinarily optimistic. Worse still, we now seem unsure whether other generations will be willing to meet the cost. The idea of the old as a marginal group in terms of generational interests developed as a significant theme over the period of the 1980s and 1990s. It is this third area in the crisis of social ageing that is discussed in the next chapter of this study.

Notes

1 These surveys are reviewed in Stevenson (1977) and Clarke (1996).

2 The fall was especially marked in the case of men. The proportion of men in occupational pension schemes fell from 64 per cent in 1983 to 57 per cent in 1991. In contrast, the proportion of women in schemes was the same in 1991 (at 37 per cent) as in 1983.

3 This aspect is also discussed in Phillipson et al. (forthcoming).

4 These findings were reinforced by a *Guardian*/ICM opinion poll carried out in 1997. This showed strong support, across all age groups, for maintaining expenditure on older people. There was particular resistance to compulsory insurance schemes to fund residential and nursing care (*Guardian*, 9 December 1997).

5 Government thinking on pensions is summarized in the Green Paper on the Welfare State (Department of Social Security, 1998) Critical perspectives on the future of pensions from the pensioners movement itself can be found in National Pensioners Convention (1998).

6 The Office of Fair Trading report on pensions found that a worker who moves several times can find his or her pension up to 30 per cent lower than someone who stays in the same scheme.

7

THE SOCIOLOGY OF GENERATIONS: CONFLICT OR CONSENSUS?

The previous two chapters explored two areas in which old age was reconstructed in the 1970s and 1980s, namely in terms of the nature of retirement and in the pattern of financial support to older people. However, another of the 'pillars' supporting elderly people also began to be questioned in this period, this relating to the support provided from younger to older generations. There have been two separate dimensions here. First, the idea of older people as a financial burden, the increasing numbers of whom are threatening to create unsustainable demands and expectations regarding benefits and services. Second, has been the theme (pursued with more vigour in the USA than the UK) of 'generational equity', or the idea that younger generations (and children in particular) are being deprived of resources going towards an increasingly affluent and wealthy generation of older people.

It is what has been described as the 'moral economy' of ageing which has come under siege over the past 10 years. What Minkler (1991) calls 'compassionate ageism' has been replaced by a view of the old as in some respects 'less deserving' than other social groups. Bengston (1993) views this development as part of what he refers to as a new social problem that has emerged in the last decades of the twentieth century. He summarizes the central features of this as follows:

> We have reached a cultural watershed concerning the implicit understanding of rights and obligations between age groups and generations in modern societies. Never before have so many elders lived so long; never before have so relatively few members of younger age groups lined up behind them in the succession of generations . . . In consequence we are faced with new and historically unique dilemmas of family life and social policy agendas regarding the expectable life course and the succession of age groups. These dilemmas are reflected in emerging questions about social welfare, both private and public, directed to age groups, as well as in more general issues of conflict and solidarity between them. Can we afford an ageing society? Can we afford to grow old in the 21st century? (1993: 4)

In fact, questions of this kind have always been part of the debate about ageing and were central to policy debates (though for different reasons) both before and just after the Second World War (Phillipson, 1982). But it is the context of these concerns that is surely making the difference as we move into a new century. The difference is that debates about ageing have merged in with wider doubts about the purpose of traditional institutions and statuses in a late modern age (Giddens, 1991). In the modern age, old age was viewed as a 'social problem' amenable to 'solutions' of different kinds: social security, the development of retirement, and support for health care. In the period of late modernity these have been called into question. Most fundamental of all are the doubts expressed about ageing as an issue that can be solved by generations working together – the idea of interdependency. From the 1980s onwards, we began to question not just whether financial arrangements were too expensive, but also whether we were producing unacceptable costs for the middle and younger generations. It is the characteristics as well as the issues arising from this debate that we explore in this chapter, focusing in particular on the complexity of the generational dimension to understanding old age.

Generations in conflict

In 1949 the Royal Commission on Population delivered its report on the long-term future of the population of Great Britain. The background to the work of the Commission was the concern, expressed throughout the decades of the thirties and forties, about the possible dangers arising from the ageing of the population. In this debate, older people were depicted as a burden on society; a group with the potential for reducing the living standards of the nation and increasing the financial pressures on future generations of workers. The Royal Commission expressed particular anxiety about the conflict of interest between workers and pensioners. The basis for this concern was expressed in the Commission's view that:

> . . . if all the old sit back on their first pensionable birthday and draw a pension with which they compete for consumer goods made by a decreasing section of the population, the standard of life of both generations will inevitably be endangered. (1949: 322)

The idea of generations competing over scarce resources was underplayed over the next two decades as Britain, in common with many other industrial societies, fashioned new approaches to the provision of welfare. However, by the 1970s and 1980s, the notion of generational conflict was back on the political agenda and had become a major topic of debate within and beyond the gerontological community (Easterlin, 1978; Clark and Spengler, 1980; Johnson et al., 1989; Thomson, 1996; Walker, 1996; Pampel, 1998). Some of the features of this debate bear similarities to that initiated by the Royal Commission over 40 years ago. Thus, in an influential article, Samuel Preston (1984) raised the possibility of direct competition between young and old over the distribution of economic resources. From a social and economic perspective, Preston argued that it was difficult to justify curtailing expenditure on children. Echoing the views of the Royal Commission, Preston (1984: 49) concluded that: 'Whereas expenditure on the elderly can be thought of mainly as consumption, expenditure on the young is a combination of consumption and investment.' Preston went on to highlight the possibility of increasing polarization in the provision of social policy, concluding:

> If we care about our collective future rather than simply about our future as individuals we are faced with the question of how best to safeguard the human and material resources represented by children. These resources have not been carefully guarded in the past two decades. (1984: 49)

A crucial element in the debate about population ageing has been the use of the concept of generations as a means of explaining both current and potential problems facing the welfare state. Older people have been depicted as a 'selfish welfare generation' (Thomson, 1989), or 'greedy geezers' (*New Republic*, 28 March 1988) in the more direct language of North Americans, soaking the young while contributing to huge public expenditure deficits.

In Britain, the idea of the old competing for scarce resources gained ground during the 1990s, this reflecting widespread anxieties about the funding of the welfare state. The political message, from a variety of sources, was that young and old were on a collision course, with youthful taxpayers likely to show increasing resistance to supporting the old. Robert Skidelsky (*The Sunday Times*, 6 July 1997) explained this development in the following terms:

> The reason is that the welfare state has become increasingly redistributive. It does not so much redistribute income from the rich to the poor as from the productive – many of whom are poor themselves – to the unproductive. A declining population of workers supports an ever-larger population of drones.

And David Walker, writing in the *Independent on Sunday* (20 July 1997), pushed the stakes somewhat higher when he portrayed a younger generation staggering from the burden of paying student loans for university education on the one side, and the need to support an ageing population on the other. From this picture he derived the following somewhat apocalyptic conclusion:

If and when they do have children the young adults of the 21st-century will be required, during their lifetimes, to find the money to support the ageing of the generation now in its forties and fifties, along with an increasing number of older survivors. Baby-boomers will start retiring during the first decade of the new century. Many will not have voluntarily provided well for their old age and will expect to be provided with increasingly expensive social services.

The issues raised by the above comments embrace conceptual as well as empirical dimensions. The former concerns questions about the difficulties involved in using the idea of generations as a basis for analysis. The latter involves examining the adequacy of the arguments themselves, and assessing the degree to which ageing populations create the kind of pressures suggested by some advocates of the 'workers versus pensioners' thesis. In what follows, we consider both these aspects, beginning with some general points that need to be taken into account when considering relationships between generations.

The concept of generations

The issues raised in the debate outlined above raise crucial questions about the issue of generations as a sociological as opposed to economic concept. Economists are right, within their own terms, to point to the problems associated with resource transfers across generations. Clearly we cannot avoid important issues regarding how resources are allocated and the likely impact on different social groups. But the question we need to pursue is whether the framing of these issues in generational terms clarifies or obscures the issues at stake. From a sociological perspective, the questions that need to be asked must include: how reliable is the idea of generations as a predictor of social and political action? Do people behave as if they are members of distinctive generations? And if they do, does this point to conflict or cooperation in the years ahead?

The first observation to be made is that an economic generation and a sociological generation are really two distinct entities. With the former, issues are presented in terms of discrete groups competing – selfishly or otherwise – for a fair share of resources. At its most extreme, this model suggests that generations behave as if on a collision course, with the block votes of the old threatening to cut off services needed by the young (Longman, 1987), and the young reconsidering the basis of the welfare contract and supporting threats to dismantle the welfare state (Thomson, 1989). This last point has been expressed by Thomson as follows:

. . . the very nature of aged populations is changing, in ways not compre-
hended in our present debates, and along with this come shifts in relations

between generations. Members of the welfare generation are now arriving at old age with assets, expectations and histories of benefits quite unlike those of their predecessors, and it remains to be seen whether the young who are expected to make growing transfers to them will feel bound to do so. At the end of the twentieth century the implicit welfare contract that binds members of successor generations is up for renegotiation – and the aged stand right at the centre of this with a great deal to lose. (1989: 35)

Of course, we might note the point made by Riley et al. (1972) that diverse tendencies do not necessarily become manifest in antagonism or erupt into organized conflict. They comment: 'The mere fact of inequality among age strata (as is true of other types of stratification also) is not a sufficient condition for age cleavage (1972: 443). In reality, the socio-logical generation will almost certainly behave in a more complex way than that suggested by the worker versus pensioner perspective. What does the sociologist mean when he or she uses the term 'generations'? Philip Abrams (1982), in a classic essay, used the definition adopted by Heberle, namely, that a generation consisted: '. . . of contemporaries of approximately the same age but for whom age is established not by the calendar of years but by a calendar of events and experiences'. Heberle concluded that: 'A generation is a phenomenon of collective mentality and morality. [The members] of a generation feel themselves linked by a community of standpoints, of beliefs and wishes' (Abrams, 1982: 258). But the extent to which people identify with a particular generation is itself a complex issue. Abrams himself points out that the cut-off points between generations are often obscure and may only develop gradually as part of a long historical process. And this point has been further developed by the US historian Andrew Achenbaum, who suggests that the meaning of the term 'generation' is 'both fuzzy and arbitrary' (1986: 93). He argues:

Less clear cut than the distinction between parent and child, the term may refer with equal plausibility to all people between certain ages, to progenitors of any age (as opposed to their progeny), and/or to people who lived through a monumental experience such as the great Depression. The very ambiguity of meaning makes it hard to know who is precisely included or excluded in such a definition. Worse, referring to people as being of a certain generation attributes to them characteristics which they may or may not possess. Who, after all, is a member of the 'gypped generation'? Where and how does one draw the line: on the basis of age? birth order? income? expectations?

This last point is of fundamental importance and was central to the position adopted by Karl Mannheim (1952) in his essay 'The problem of generations'. Contrary to much of the present speculation about the possible behaviour of generations, Mannheim noted that the character-istic of what he termed 'generational units' was that their location and effectiveness in social systems could not be explained adequately on the basis of age alone. Following this, Abrams writes that:

> Age is a necessary but not a sufficient condition for their existence. Other factors such as class, religion, race, occupation, institutional setting, in short all the conventional categories of social-structural analysis, must be introduced to explain their unique ability to make something of historical experiences. In other words, the study of generations brings to light consequential differ- entiations within generations as well as between them. Far from exempting us from the study of social structure any attempt to grapple with the problem of the historical formation of identity forces us in just that direction. The emergence of generation units and their capacity or inability to reconstruct identity can only be explained in those terms. Here as elsewhere historical sociology means more work, not less. (1982: 261–2)

The above arguments suggest that caution is necessary when using the idea of generations to explain and predict aspects of social and political life. Unfortunately, this point has often been ignored by research in this area, hence the somewhat alarmist perspectives adopted in some of the writing and research. Having outlined some of the conceptual issues which need to be taken into account, we can now examine some of the central arguments of the 'worker versus pensioner' debate, assessing the evidence for the possibility of conflict between age groups in the years ahead.

Workers versus pensioners: the arguments reviewed

The argument about the emerging conflict between older and younger generations is built around a number of propositions. These have been set out in some detail by David Thomson (1989) in a paper entitled 'The welfare state and generational conflict: winners and losers'. The 'win- ners', according to Thomson, are older people who have been able to 'capture' the welfare state and design it in a way which ensures that their own needs are adequately met. Conversely, the 'losers' are younger people who, asked to pay out an increasingly large share of their income to support older people, will find that there is very little left for themselves when they reach retirement age. At the same time, it is argued that benefits for older people continue to expand, the growth in the income of the old outstripping that of younger people with families. Using the example of New Zealand (data from which are used to speculate about trends in Europe and the USA), Thomson finds that the single-income young family of two children now had, by the 1980s,

20 per cent less real purchasing power than it did in 1960; conversely, the elderly had 100 per cent more.

It is also suggested that younger people are themselves becoming more aware of the extent to which they are being denied resources and are working for a future which cannot be properly financed. According to Thomson, 'The young, whatever their income levels, have been learning some important lessons about their welfare state in the 1970s and 1980s – that it does not deliver, and that it has no intention of giving them what older citizens once enjoyed' (1989: 44). As a consequence, it is argued that younger people may rebel from a welfare contract which seems to work against their interests and will support policies aimed at a fundamental restructuring of the welfare state. Paul Johnson and his colleagues argue that the outcome of this will be increasing conflict between generations which: 'may affect not just the relative welfare of the old and the young, but [may] also threaten the very existence of state welfare systems' (1989: 7).

At the same time, the viability of the welfare state is itself seen to be threatened by the sheer weight of numbers of older people. According to Johnson et al.:

> It seems inevitable that the interaction of current demographic trends and current welfare policies will impose a large, growing and possibly unsustainable burden on the productive populations in developed nations. Since there can be no immediate change in the population age structure, and a rise in fertility would only raise still further the number of 'dependants', at least in the short run, it may seem that an obvious way to cope with the rising financial burden of an ageing population is to alter in some way the welfare contract that operates to transfer resources from the young to the 'old'. (1989: 9)

From the above summary, the following steps in the argument may be identified:

1 that older people have been active in designing a welfare state which works largely for their own benefit;
2 that younger people now perceive this to be the case and are beginning to act as a generational group in opposing inequities in welfare resources;
3 that the growth in the number of older people is itself a factor in generating economic instability.

Each of these arguments will be examined and its validity assessed in the context of the available evidence.

A welfare state for older people?

First, to what extent is it the case that older people have constructed a welfare state largely for their own benefit? An initial observation that might be made of this argument is that it simply ignores the weight of historical evidence about the origins of areas such as pension and welfare reform. To take just two examples: older people were not the main influences behind legislation such as the American Social Security Act of 1935 or the British Contributory Pension Act of 1925 (when the retirement age was reduced from 70 to 65). Instead, it was the impetus provided by economic depression and the view that older workers could be sacrificed to maintain employment for those with families (Graebner, 1980; Phillipson, 1982). In the post-war period it might be observed that, in the case of the USA, pressure groups representing older people (or indeed the middle aged) played a limited role either in the expansion of social security benefits or in opposing subsequent cut-backs (Graebner, 1980; Pratt, 1993). As regards Britain, it would be difficult to sustain the view that the rapid onset of early exit from the labour force (from the late 1970s) was devised by middle-aged workers seeking greater security and prosperity. In fact, the extent of job loss among the middle aged and young elderly suggests that once again it was older people who were being asked to bear the brunt of high unemployment and deflationary economic policies (Laczko and Phillipson, 1991). Moreover, the argument that the majority of these older workers were protected by a generous welfare state is also at variance with data on income support for the early retired. This suggests, in fact, a considerable degree of income inequality among those taking earlier retirement with, for many, earlier retirement meaning an extension of the years likely to be spent in poverty (Laczko, 1990).

But let us assume that it was middle-aged and older people who had been active in constructing a welfare state for their own benefit. The observation that might then be made is that this must be a rare example of an interest group forming an institution which actually entails a drop in their economic and social status (Walker, 1981; Townsend, 1981). Even if we were to accept the argument that the majority of older people were no longer disadvantaged, this could not be sustained about the post-war experience as a whole. Indeed, Thomson has himself put forward the view that if we take the value of the state pension, the elderly are substantially worse off now than they were in Victorian times (Thomson, 1996). And, according to another line of argument, retirement is one of the main factors behind the social creation of dependency in old age, with the risk of poverty three times greater for those above the retirement age than for those below it (Walker, 1993). If these arguments are correct, then it would seem that rather than behaving 'selfishly' (as is the claim from Thomson), older people have in fact been remarkably selfless in constructing a welfare state which gives them a level of participation substantially below that of many other social groups.

Finally, it must also be said that the broader argument that welfare state expenditure as a whole has favoured the old at the expense of the young, must be treated with some degree of caution. The evidence suggests that the distribution of welfare state expenditure between younger and older people is in fact roughly equal. The data here, in terms of the advantages and disadvantages of particular birth cohorts, have been summarized by Hills as follows:

> First it does appear that those born between 1901 and 1921 will end up getting rather more out the welfare state than they put in, although even this generation will have 'paid for' between 80 per cent and 90 per cent of what they get out under most assumptions . . . Secondly, it is not possible to reach conclusions about later cohorts unless one makes some kind of projection of what will happen to them in the future. If one assumes that education, health and social security will . . . maintain their current values in relation to contemporary living standards over the next 50 years, cohorts between 1921 and 1966 will end up roughly breaking even, generally making small gains . . . However, if social security payments continued to be price- rather than income-linked over the next 50 years, the picture would deteriorate for those born after 1921, and all the subsequent cohorts . . . would end up as net losers, albeit narrowly (they still get back more than 90 per cent of what they would have 'put in'). (1996: 78)

In general, attempting to argue that one generation is a clear 'winner' and another a clear 'loser' finds very little empirical validation. Moreover, even if it was possible to develop a discussion with evidence of this kind, there would still be the sociological problems identified earlier concerning the complex ways in which generations are stratified by factors such as gender, ethnicity and social class.

Attitudes towards the welfare state

The second step in the argument by David Thomson (and one shared by a number of academics as well as politicians) is that younger people are beginning to question the value of supporting a welfare state which is likely to offer them a limited range of benefits in their old age. The difficulty with this suggestion is that there is no empirical evidence to sustain the view either that younger people feel a lessening in their obligations towards the welfare state or that older people are blamed for the crisis in funding. On the former, large-scale data sets such as those of the regular series on British Social Attitudes, which have asked the public about priorities for social spending, are consistent in showing a high level of support (across all age groups) for spending on the core welfare services (Hancock et al., 1995). The Eurobarometer survey for 1993, found that the UK was fourth among EU states in its support for raising taxes to help pay for pensions. British Social Attitudes Survey data suggest a steady increase between 1983 and 1991 in the declared preference for higher spending on education, health and social benefits at the expense of increased taxation. This trend cuts across age, gender and social class differences (Hancock et al., 1995).

In the USA, the notion of a 'generational war' over support for the old is not substantiated by the relevant data. Minkler and Robertson (1991) argue that, contrary to media claims, there has been no outcry from younger taxpayers about the high costs of Social Security and Medicare (see also Marmor et al., 1990). They note that an analysis of some 20 national surveys, conducted by Louis Harris and Associates over a two-year period in the 1980s, found no validation for the intergenerational conflict hypothesis. Minkler and Robertson found from their analysis that while the elderly appeared somewhat more supportive of pro-grammes targeted at them than did younger age groups, and vice versa, the balance of attitudes in all generations was solidly on the same side. The great majority of both elderly people and young people aged under 30 thus opposed increasing monthly premiums for Medicare coverage, opposed increasing the deductible for Medicare coverage of doctors' bills, and opposed freezing Social Security cost-of-living increases. Similarly, both young and old Americans opposed cutting federal spending on education and student loans, and overwhelmingly opposed cutting federal health programmes for women and children. Minkler and Robertson conclude that: 'In short, issues of government spending and legislation affecting persons at different life stages appeared to invoke intergenerational consensus rather than conflict, in keeping with strong moral economy notions of reciprocity over the life course' (1991: 16).

The burden of older people

The third major strand in the argument is that the sheer number of 'non-productive' elderly represents a major problem for western economies. Here we should note at the outset the timeless nature both of the arguments and the language used to describe older people. Nearly 40 years separate the following observations, both roughly making the same point about the burden of old age:

> The growing increase in the proportion of older persons in the population will inevitably mean an increase in the amount of current production required for

their maintenance. The cost must not be recognized only in terms of family help towards their support or of the proportion of the pension that comes from public funds, but in terms of their contribution to the community's production and services. (Phillips Report, 1954: 11)

An inevitable corollary of this reduction in the number of years spent in employment is an increase in the length of life spent dependent on the effort and output of that section of the population currently engaged in productive work . . . Whether the retired population is supported from its own savings or from state pension and welfare payments does not affect the general proposition that the present consumption of the aged (and children) is provided for by the current output of productive workers. (Johnson et al., 1989: 4)

What is interesting about these statements is that they are operating in very similar contexts: first, a perception that the problem of poverty among older people is now confined to a minority; second, an associated view that the incomes of retired people are now 'on a par with [those] of non-aged persons' (Thomson, 1989: 52); third, an experience of labour shortages which is seen to undermine the legitimacy of retirement.

Such historical consistencies do not invalidate views about the economic problems generated by population change; they do suggest, however, that we are dealing with a question not simply of political economy, but also an ideological assessment about the place and value of older people in society. This point can be further illustrated by simply noting that, in the case of Britain, in terms of 'dependants' (that is, young as well as old) the ratio of this group to that of the economically active is virtually the same at the end of the twentieth century as it was at the beginning. In this context Bartley et al. make the point that:

The remarkably similar total dependency ratios . . . need to be seen in relation to the prodigious increase in industrial productivity which has occurred between these dates. Taken together, they suggest that the 'problem of the ageing population' concerns not inadequate resources but complex issues of the social division of responsibility for children and infirm elderly people. (1997: 77)

Let us though try to make some assessment of the long-term impact of demographic trends: will the ageing of our population in the future so adversely affect the relative size of the labour force and/or its productivity as to reduce both economic growth and improvements in the standard of living? Part of the worker versus pensioner argument rests on particular scenarios about the direction of population change, and the move towards smaller cohorts of workers supporting large cohorts of retirees (World Bank, 1994). However, the trends here are complex and subject to considerable variation across the industrialized world. This point was illustrated by the OECD (1988) report on the social policy implications of ageing populations. Taking, for example, 'total dependency ratios' (that is, the number of older people (aged 65+), and young (aged 0–14) persons, relative to those of working age), the basic trends for the period 1980–2050, for selected countries, are illustrated in Table 7.1. On average, the total dependency ratio is projected to increase by 19 per cent between 1980 and 2040, when it generally peaks. The variation between the OECD countries is, however, substantial. The report notes that the ratio is expected to decline in Ireland and Turkey, to increase by 10 per cent or less in New Zealand, Portugal and the UK, and to increase by over 30 per cent in Canada, Germany, Japan and the Netherlands.

After 2010, however, the report notes a substantial rise in the dependency ratio for virtually all countries as the proportion of older people

Table 7.1   *Total dependency ratios in OECD countries, 1980–2050*

	1980	1990	2000	2010	2020	2030	2040	2050	% Change	
									1980–2040	2010–2040
Canada	48.1	47.4	47.9	46.6	55.3	66.5	68.4	67.7	42	47
France	56.8	51.8	52.6	50.8	57.3	64.4	68.3	68.2	20	34
Germany	50.8	44.0	48.3	50.5	54.3	68.7	74.8	69.9	47	48
Italy	54.9	46.1	47.9	48.6	51.5	61.1	69.9	67.6	27	44
Japan	48.4	42.2	48.6	58.6	60.6	59.5	66.8	65.7	38	14
United Kingdom	56.2	51.9	53.8	52.7	56.7	61.9	62.1	60.2	10	18
United States	51.1	51.6	49.8	47.2	54.6	62.4	63.1	62.5	23	34
Average of the above	52.3	47.9	49.9	50.7	55.8	63.5	67.6	66.0	29	34
Australia	53.5	49.9	49.5	48.2	52.9	59.5	63.0	63.0	18	31
Austria	56.2	48.5	50.9	52.5	56.7	66.6	70.2	66.5	25	34
Belgium	52.4	49.2	49.3	48.0	51.6	60.2	64.4	63.7	23	34
Denmark	54.5	47.3	44.3	45.7	51.8	61.5	70.3	68.9	29	54
Finland	47.7	47.8	46.8	48.4	59.9	67.1	67.7	68.5	42	40
Greece	56.1	48.3	51.3	53.3	54.1	58.0	61.9	62.6	10	16
Iceland	59.8	54.8	48.2	42.9	46.9	57.5	64.3	66.7	7	50
Ireland	70.0	63.5	52.4	47.3	48.5	54.1	60.2	63.2	−14	27
Luxembourg	47.8	47.3	52.6	52.0	58.1	65.6	65.3	63.4	37	26
Netherlands	51.1	44.5	46.3	46.1	53.1	64.8	69.6	66.2	36	51
New Zealand	58.0	49.4	47.6	45.7	50.0	58.4	63.8	63.4	10	40
Norway	58.5	53.6	50.7	47.9	53.3	61.0	67.4	66.4	15	41
Portugal	58.6	52.1	53.7	51.1	51.4	57.3	62.3	62.0	6	22
Spain	58.1	52.5	51.9	47.8	49.0	58.4	68.4	69.0	18	43
Sweden	56.0	53.7	51.5	52.5	59.0	63.2	66.4	65.0	19	26
Switzerland	50.5	46.1	49.6	54.6	63.6	73.1	76.5	73.7	52	40
Turkey	78.1	65.9	59.1	49.0	47.3	54.3	56.7	51.9	−27	16
OECD average	55.6	50.4	50.2	49.5	54.1	61.9	66.3	65.7	19	35

Note
[Population (aged 0–14) + (aged 65+)/population aged 15–64] × 100. 1980 are actual ratios; those for 1990 to 2050 are projected ratios.

Source: OECD (1988)

increases. The exceptions to this pattern are Turkey, where the ratio is projected to continue falling until after 2020, and countries such as Ireland and Spain where it is not expected to rise significantly until after 2020. In the case of Japan and the UK, the projected increases in the ratio for the period between 2010 and 2040 is also relatively small.

These variations have important implications in terms of financial support for older people. Regarding Britain, the relatively gradual change in the ratio actually presents an excellent opportunity to provide a secure framework of financial and social support for old age. Hills (1995: 38) argues that despite the rhetoric associated with talk of a 'demographic timebomb', the pressure on welfare spending is significantly smaller than in other comparable countries. He argues:

> In the British case, ageing will put pressure on social security and health budgets, but the level of pressure leaves open the political choice as to whether to cope through higher taxes and national insurance payments, or by reducing provision for particular needs below the current level of provision in relation to contemporary incomes. Other countries face much more painful versions of the same choice.

An additional point to note is that adapting to alterations in worker–pensioner ratios has already been successfully achieved in many countries, a point illustrated in Table 7.2. Indeed, the change in such ratios between, for example, 1960 and 1980, was for many of a similar magnitude to that predicted for the opening decades of the twenty-first century. Clearly, though, the secular trend is of considerable significance and raises many important issues. In particular, will the development of a smaller workforce, servicing an expanding elderly population, retard economic growth? Will the tax burden on the working population undermine incentives in respect of work and investment?

Table 7.2   *Ratio of persons aged 15–64 to persons aged 65 and over*

	1960	1980	2000	2025	Ratio 1980/ 1960	Ratio 2025/ 2000
Austria	5.46	4.17	4.27	2.87	0.764	0.672
Belgium	5.41	4.57	4.05	2.95	0.845	0.729
Finland	8.70	5.65	4.74	2.77	0.649	0.584
France	5.32	4.57	4.24	3.01	0.859	0.711
Greece	7.94	4.88	3.89	3.01	0.615	0.774
Italy	7.04	4.90	4.02	2.90	0.696	0.722
Luxembourg	6.25	5.00	4.33	2.66	0.800	0.614
Netherlands	6.76	5.75	4.85	2.65	0.851	0.545
Norway	5.68	4.27	4.17	3.00	0.752	0.721
Spain	7.81	5.88	4.39	3.38	0.753	0.770
Sweden	5.52	3.94	3.72	2.60	0.714	0.701
United Kingdom	5.56	4.26	4.24	3.12	0.766	0.735

Source: Adapted from Ermisch (1990: 45)

In fact, there may be a number of reasons for questioning whether changes to the worker–pensioner ratio has negative economic effects. First, the impact of a change in the ratio has to be related to overall levels of employment. For example, the International Labour Organisation (1989) argues that the UK will be able to cushion the effect of an ageing population by continuing to cut levels of unemployment. Thus, if employment remained at the level it was in 1985, the ratio of non-employed persons (those retired plus the unemployed) to the economically active would increase 23.2 per cent by 2025. If, on the other hand, unemployment was eradicated, this dependency ratio would actually fall by 16.7 per cent (ILO, 1989).

Second, the argument that population ageing will have a damaging effect on productivity needs to be examined with equal caution. In a detailed assessment of this issue in the context of the US economy, Palmer and Gould (1986) put forward some predictions about the impact of demographic change on per capita economic growth. They used four main variables: labour force to population growth; capital per worker; labour quality and efficiency; and technological change. Palmer and Gould note a number of positive features about demographic change which might also be transposed to other economies: first, that, as observed above, dependency ratios will not substantially 'deteriorate' until we are into the second decade of the twenty-first century; second, that during this period (and for a variety of reasons) there will be a greater concentration of capital per worker and therefore, all things being equal, more output per worker; third, that the general ageing of the labour force over a broad range of occupations will increase its overall productivity; fourth, that there will be improved prospects for increasing the quantity and quality of general education and training per worker. The authors conclude that even on the basis of somewhat pessimistic estimates about future population growth: '[such change] should no more inhibit rising standards of living over the next 50 years than it has in the past' (Palmer and Gould, 1986: 373).

In short, apocalyptic views about too many elderly causing a threat to the viability of western economies must, for the moment, be suspended. At the same time, we might put forward another type of argument: namely, that the pessimism from Thomson and others is partly due to somewhat restricted notions of productivity. Here, Neugarten and Neugarten make the point that:

> . . . the ageing society will need a broader definition of productivity than the one current today, a definition that goes beyond participation in the labour force and extends to non-paid roles. These would include not only those that are attached to formally organised voluntary associations, but also to services that individuals provide to family members both inside and outside the household, services to neighbours and friends, and self-care activities. The need is to seek out and nurture the potential for social productivity, in this

broad sense, wherever it is to be found – not only among the young-old, but among younger people as well. (1986: 48)

In fact, it is precisely in the area of social relations within the family that we are seeing new patterns of generational behaviour, ones which give a different picture to the idea of a 'selfish' and demanding welfare generation.

Older people and the welfare state: changes within the family

One further question mark against the idea of generational conflict is that it ignores changes to other areas within the welfare state, in particular that relating to the family. For example, an extension of the generational conflict idea might be that just as older people are failing to moderate claims at the macro-level of the welfare system, they are also exerting undue pressure at the micro-level of the family. According to this line of reasoning, the numerous reports from studies of the plight of carers might be one indication of the way in which older people have continued to receive a disproportionate share not only of state support, but also of that arising from informal care of different kinds. Does the evidence support such an interpretation? In fact, there are some data now available which suggest that older people are altering the claims which they make on the family, and that we are seeing new attitudes beginning to emerge about the relative merits of formal as opposed to informal support.

The dominant sociological view, for a number of years, has been that, as Shanas asserts: 'old persons turn first to their families for help, then to neighbours and finally to the bureaucratic agencies and others, because they expect families to help in case of need' (Shanas, 1979: 174). And Wenger concludes from her review that 'Research . . . demonstrates that not only does most care come from the family but that most people think that this is where the responsibility should lie' (1984: 14).

This view has of course been central to the philosophy of community care, both in Britain and elsewhere. However, it can be argued that there is no consistent evidence to support this perspective. Indeed, research is now available which suggests that care preferences are changing and that this reflects an important shift in the relationship between older people and the family. The argument here is that there is a re-adjustment in attitudes towards receiving and, to a lesser extent, giving care. The implication of this is that the hidden welfare state is shrinking: in part because of fewer carers in the relevant age and gender group (women aged 45–60); but, in addition, because of changes in attitudes and expectations on the part of older people themselves. What evidence is there for such change on the part of older people in Britain?

In terms of care preferences, some of the key points can be summarized in the following way: first, we should note the public opinion surveys which show the extent to which adults of all ages focus on the state, rather than the family, in respect of needs for financial, health and social support (Salvage et al., 1989; Phillipson, 1990). A Gallup survey carried out in the late 1980s found that most pensioners believed that responsibility for their care *should shift towards that of the state*. Out of 909 people aged 65 plus who were interviewed, 57 per cent overall expressed this view (*Guardian*, 22 November 1988). A survey reported by Parker and Clarke (1997) investigated the attitudes and behaviour of men and women aged 25 to 70 years regarding financial planning for care in old age. This found that most people believe that the state should take primary responsibility for the provision of older people's care, and that this was financially affordable. Although there was support for the idea of help being means-related, people were found to be somewhat reluctant to use available means (such as capital tied up in housing) to fund their own care.

West et al. (1984) explored views about the care of dependent groups and the relationship between the state, professional groups and informal carers. They found from their study that: '. . . the public are unwilling to place the major burden of care on informal carers which in practice means the family and women in particular. They are especially unwilling to allocate the major responsibility for care to close kin; the children or siblings of dependent persons' (West et al., 1984: 294).

In contrast, a 1996 survey of public opinion found most people who were not currently carers expected that their family or friends would look after them if they could no longer look after themselves. However, although the greatest burden was seen to fall upon the family, more than six out of ten of the (non-carer) general public believe that the state should pay the major share of the cost of care – 45 per cent feeling that central government, and 17 per cent that local councils should pay the major share. Less than three in ten (28 per cent) felt that the cost should be shared fairly evenly between the family and the state. A very small proportion (less than 5 per cent) believed that the cost of this care should fall primarily upon the cared-for person and their family (Carers National Association, 1996)

It might be argued that findings on care preferences reflect important changes in the lifestyles and attitudes of older people over the last 20 to 30 years (Fennell et al., 1988). These changes have received some recognition in proposals for community care, particularly with the emphasis on maintaining people in their own homes, as well as providing greater choice in the provision of services (Department of Health, 1989). But acknowledgement of changes in attitudes towards the giving and receiving of family care has yet to be followed to its logical conclusion: namely, that older people are moving away from wanting any dependence on children, especially that which implies a long-term commitment arising out of a chronic illness (Lee, 1985) or the need to provide personal care (Ungerson, 1987).

The arguments about changing care preferences are highlighted by research on patterns of kinship obligations. Janet Finch (1989) has highlighted the complex set of rules determining the provision of family care. She notes that kin relationships do not operate on the basis of a ready-made set of moral rules, clearly laid out for older people and their carers to follow. In particular, the 'sense of obligation' which marks the distinctive character of kin relations does not follow a reliable and consistent path in terms of social practice. Finch writes:

> It is actually much less reliable than that. It is nurtured and grows over time between some individuals more strongly than others, and its practical consequences are highly variable. It does have a binding quality, but that derives from commitments built up between real people over many years, not from an abstract set of moral values. (1989: 242)

This argument is important because it cuts across a central thrust of state policy in Britain on community care, namely that families act as though there are cultural and moral scripts which they follow in supporting older people in times of crisis or dependency. Moreover, the argument is taken a stage further by some researchers with the assertion that older people themselves follow this path, with an almost instinctive tendency to move towards the family rather than bureaucratic agencies. Such arguments, however, rely upon a historical perspective which may no longer be acceptable as an accurate portrayal of the kind of care wanted by people. Families are variable in their response to requests for help and, in any event, the care given is always negotiated within a social and biographical context (Finch 1989). It is this variability which makes the future of family care in Britain somewhat uncertain. People may come to prefer (may indeed demand) the provision of a reliable network of public sector services (supported by other providers such as the private and not-for-profit sectors), these replacing the hitherto dominant role of family and informal sector care.

According to this perspective, family care in the 1990s and beyond, although still present – and stronger in some social groups than others – will alter in terms both of the conditions under which care is provided and the range of care tasks that can be performed. The empirical evidence suggests in fact that older people may be reassessing the kind of demands they can make within the family. The consequence of this – in intergenerational terms – may be to free family members to engage in different kinds of productive activities and for the total adult time devoted to children to increase. Both these points need to be born in mind when trends in welfare support for young and old are examined.

Alternative approaches

A number of criticisms have been advanced in this chapter regarding the possibilities of conflict between generations over population ageing. Three additional points might be made to further illustrate the limitations of conventional approaches in this area. First, we need to start questioning many of the assumptions made in extrapolations from changes in dependency ratios. For example, it is assumed that aged dependants will represent a greater per capita cost than young dependants. However, some economists have questioned the adequacy of current information on the relative costs of young and old people. Schultz (1980), for example, cites a West German study which found that the total cost of rearing a child to the age of 20 is a quarter to a third higher than the cost of supporting a 60-year-old for the rest of his/her life.

Second, and more importantly, we perhaps need to start revising the traditional way in which dependency ratios are calculated. Typically, we use segmental ratios (comparing the population aged 65 and over with that aged 18–64) or dependency ratios (comparing the numbers of workers to non-workers). But a more satisfactory approach may be to take a wider definition of productivity and include within the productive age group persons aged 65–74. This might be justified on the basis of the contributions made by this group to the maintenance of family and community life, as well as of the direct contribution of a minority to the economy (in various forms of part-time and self-employment) . Using this approach, and given that the majority of persons in this age group can live independently in the community, we are likely to produce more optimistic scenarios of future demographic trends than traditional approaches would suggest (see Friedmann and Adamchak, 1983, for a discussion along these lines).

Third, it might be observed that in making predictions into the twenty-first century it is important to recognize wider political, cultural and social transformations which might modify the changes under discussion. For example, the argument in the study by Johnson et al. (1989) assumes that economies will continue to operate largely within national boundaries. Yet it is barely conceivable, given the pace of change in the European community for example, that this will be the case. In fact, the possibilities for much more permeable national boundaries and hence labour markets are such that we might envisage the flexible transfer of workers to areas where particular skills are in short supply (something which is already beginning to happen).[1] Such developments will allow us to modify, albeit in a modest way, some of the more pessimistic assumptions about the impact of demographic change.

Conclusion

This chapter has summarized a number of the arguments which might be developed in challenging some of the more alarmist views about demographic change. Constructing the intellectual arguments, however, is one thing; challenging their insidious effect on the lives of older people is rather more complex. The fact is that the ideological pressure upon older people has been at least as damaging as the changes in work patterns and financial support discussed earlier. Taken together, these areas represent a major transformation in terms of the frameworks which have traditionally been relied upon to support older people. This point is less easy to see when each of these structures is analysed separately. Viewed together, however, we can see more clearly the way in which growing old has been reshaped by the institutions of a late or post-modern society. In the next chapter we shall use the arguments explored in Part II to provide a general overview of the lives of older people in the twentieth century.

Note

1 European Union legislation in 1998 started moves towards portability of private pensions within the Union. The object of this being to facilitate the migration of workers across member states.

PART III

NEW AGENDAS

8

OLD AGE: SOCIOLOGICAL AND HISTORICAL PERSPECTIVES

Part II reviewed the various ways in which old age was transformed in the decades of the 1980s and the 1990s. The changes affecting areas such as retirement, pensions and relationships between generations have raised major issues about the status of older people at the close of the twentieth century. The gains and benefits of an ageing society seem increasingly open to question. Thomas Cole has expressed this point in relation to the USA as follows:

> By the late 1970s, a spectre was haunting the United States – the spectre of an ageing society. Awareness that the national population was ageing blended silently into fears of nuclear holocaust, environmental deterioration, military and economic decline, social conflict and cultural decadence . . . Youthful optimism and belief in limitless progress . . . appeared increasingly incongruous in a society confronting limits on all sides. (1992: 233–4)

Increasingly, the issue has become one of how to make sense of human life where survival into old age is combined with release from the need for productive employment. The former points to the demographic triumph of the twentieth century. As Peter Clarke (1996) observes, for Britain at the beginning of the century, old age came 10 years (for men) and 20 years (for women) sooner than it does now. He writes: 'Only after the age of sixty-five did a woman in 1980 have less than a 99 per cent chance of surviving the next year, whereas in 1900 a woman had the same expectation from as early as her forty-fifth birthday' (1996: 40).

But longevity has come alongside another important development: namely, that in industrial societies a majority of the population are no longer required for paid employment. Hobsbawm expresses this point as follows:

> . . . for most of the industrial era the production of manufactured goods and services, even when it was not labour intensive, required a vast and growing labour force, but at present that is rapidly ceasing to be the case. For the first time in history, it is no longer necessary that the bulk of humanity must in the biblical phrase, 'eat thy bread in the sweat of thy face'. (1997: 21)

The dilemmas and anxieties about ageing revolve, in most respects, around the interplay between these elements – two of the most important aspects of what Hobsbawm (1994) has elsewhere characterized as the 'short twentieth century'. At the end of this century, it is equally clear that we remain unsure about precisely how to handle the social and economic changes that have followed on from the maturing of population structures on the one side, and industrial societies on the other. A hundred years ago problems of ageing were resolved by a combination of premature death and the need to work. Now, changes in public health have significantly challenged the former (though significant class-related inequalities remain), and retirement has opened a significant space for personal development after the ending of work. But neither of these changes appears to have been easily assimilated. Indeed, as we move into a new century, the problems and tensions associated with population ageing seem even less clear as regards their resolution.

The purpose of this and the following chapter is to summarize and review some of the main arguments developed in this book, and to assess as well the basis for alternative social policies for old age. The focus of this chapter is on providing a broad framework for interpreting the main changes that have affected older people during the twentieth century.

The politics of resentment

The previous chapter charted the growth in what has been referred to as 'apocalyptic demography' (Robertson, 1991) or 'the politics of resentment' (Turner, 1989). Regardless of which label is applied, attitudes to demographic change have been significant in reshaping what might be termed the 'moral landscape of ageing'. Older people, it would seem, no longer have an inalienable right to given health and financial resources. This view has been spelt out most clearly by medical ethicists such as Daniel Callahan (1987), in books such as *Setting Limits: Medical Goals in an Aging Society*. Here, Callahan suggests three aspirations for an ageing society: first, to stop pursuing medical goals that combine the features of high costs, marginal gains, and benefits (in the main) for the old; second, that the old shift their priorities from their own welfare to that of younger generations; and third, that older people should accept death as a condition of life, at least for the sake of others. Callahan argues in fact that:

> . . . it is only through toughly and energetically embracing old age as a time of both service to the future and decline and withdrawal that its value as a stage in life can ultimately be redeemed. (1987: 49)

This is not the place to provide a general critique of Callahan's position, and in any event this has already been developed elsewhere (see, especially, Homer and Holstein, 1990; Binstock and Post, 1991; Moody, 1992). Of more relevance is an argument that underpins Callahan's work, from which he draws somewhat questionable conclusions, but which is important and relevant to the concerns of this book. In particular, Callahan adopts a critical stance towards what he calls the 'modernization of ageing'. By this he means:

> . . . the belief that the physical process of ageing ought to be aggressively resisted, and that the life of the aged ought to be transformed from one of old-fashioned disengagement and preparation for death to a continuingly active involvement in life and a persistent struggle against decay and demise. (1987: 26)

Callahan identifies a further set of beliefs as follows:

> A more recent [view] has been that because of the rapid pace of social change, the future is best left in the hands of the energetic and adaptable young. The modernization of ageing represents a still more advanced stage: to be old is to be potentially (if not quite yet) better than to be young because it is the new frontier of medical progress, of personal freedom and individualism, and of styles of life that could transform industrial societies. Under this dispensation, the aged are not at all a surplus group, or merely 'senior citizens' serving out their time until death. They are the new pioneers. The kind of healthy, self-directing, self-realizing, past-transcending life they are now in principle able to live becomes the medical, social, and political goal, the ultimate reward of a progressive and medically enlightened society. (1987: 27)

Callahan's view is that not all of this philosophy is wrong, rather that in presenting the issues in this way we duck hard thinking (and choices) about the meaning and purpose of later life. He concludes:

> There is nothing in that modernizing aspiration which promises to respond to the present root problem of ageing, that of the need for a respected place for old age in society and in the lives of individuals. It may actually have created new problems, at once offering no real alternative for the aged but to follow the crowd in their struggle against old age while at the same time draining resources from other societal needs. (1987: 29)

Leaving aside the final point, it might be argued that Callahan's view about the 'root problem of ageing' is actually rather limited. The basis for his view seems to be that it is the *ideas* of modernity which are the problem, these failing to address some of the fundamental concerns and issues which accompany ageing. We would certainly agree that ideas are important and that those associated with old age have become somewhat impoverished. However, the explanation for this may be attributed, first, to the collapse of some of the key institutions and practices associated with modernity – notably those relating to retirement and the welfare state. Second, to the processes associated with 'late modernity' (see Chapter 4), with the unfolding of a chronic sense of insecurity and anxiety among groups such as older women and older men.

This is not to suggest that there is anything quintessentially new about old age as a period of crisis: the history of old age is almost certainly one of a continual battle for support within and outside the family unit (Laslett, 1983). Rather, the 'newness' is partly the dialectic between the triumph of demography and industry – which is essentially a triumph of the second half of the twentieth century; partly, also, this is an issue associated with the move into a new stage of modernity, as identified by Giddens, Beck and other social scientists.

For older people the nature of the crisis revolves around the way in which the unravelling of 'institutional identities' has exposed fundamental concerns about personal identity itself. Here we part company with biographical perspectives on ageing, as discussed in Chapter 2, in the sense that there is rather more to identity than the narratives or stories that people carry into this phase of the life course. Such stories are themselves embedded in wider layers of meaning, these emerging from social and economic practices at large within society. People search for meaning and reinforcement of their stories 'outside' as well as 'inside' themselves. People age 'from within' in a double sense: 'within' themselves and 'within' society. The crisis of social ageing essentially concerns the disjunction between the two, with the social meanings attached to growing old in tension with ageing as a psychological and biographical event.

The construction of old age: 1900–1930

It is important to give some additional clarification to the nature of the concerns being raised here. The question that needs to be asked in studies of ageing (but one which is rarely asked) is: what is it that constitutes being an older person; or as Katz expresses it: '. . . how did elderly people *become the elderly*'. Katz goes on to observe that:

To be old merely requires that one ages. However, to be part of a population of elderly persons requires that one be absorbed into a specific discourse of differentiation. (1996: 51)

This idea of the old as a separate group in the population actually only emerged at the end of the nineteenth century. Prior to this, as Slater (1930) notes in his history of policies towards the poor, provision for old age was not at first differentiated from provision for sickness. In his account of the role of friendly societies and trade unions, Slater argues that it was only towards the end of the nineteenth century that the societies found themselves obliged to rule that sickness benefit should be ended at the age of 65, and then be replaced by an old age pension. At this point, the political environment began to focus on old age as a 'problem' requiring new social policies (Phillipson, 1978; Achenbaum, 1978; Quadagno, 1986; Katz, 1996). In the USA, Fischer dates what he sees as the 'discovery' of ageing as a social issue from around 1910, identifying the following landmarks:

Recognition of ageing appeared in the first public commission on ageing (Massachusetts, 1909), and the first major survey of the economic condition of the aged (Massachusetts again, 1910); in the first federal old age pension bill (1909), and the first state old age pension system (Arizona, 1915); in the invention of a new science named geriatrics (1909); and the first published textbook in that field (1914). (1977: 157)

In Britain, discussion about the provision of state pensions began in the 1870s, with legislation for non-contributory pensions coming in 1908 (Thane, 1978). Older people were also a significant group identified in the classic surveys of poverty by Booth and Rowntree, and also featuring in studies of unemployment by Chapman and Hallsworth (1909), and Rowntree and Lasker (1911).

From the first two decades of the twentieth century, then, older people emerged as a group differentiated in terms of the nature of their poverty as well their marginal status in relation to regular work. By the age of 70, one Edwardian in five was a pauper; and of those who lived to 75, almost one in three. Thompson notes: 'An old person's chances of actually dying in the workhouse in the years before a national health service were even higher' (1975: 83–4).

Becoming an elderly person was, then, to enter a stage in life where poverty and marginalization were a common occurrence. This experience was crucial in determining the framework within which older age was constructed. On the one side were the 'popular and negative definitions of the elderly as a problem population' (Katz, 1996: 57; see also Cole, 1992), an image reinforced by the clusters of (mainly) aged women residing within workhouse institutions (Longmate, 1974). On the other side was a less punitive view of the old, one that focused on their 'deserving' of a reward for past contributions to society (Novack, 1988).

Crucially, the construction of old age is built around 'harsh' or 'softer' versions of dependency. Flora Thompson's (1973 [1945]) record of the 'tears of gratitude' from older people in a Cotswold village when receiving their first pension, set the scene for a recurring image in the twentieth century: the old as beneficiaries of state, voluntary and private charity. No matter that the 1908 pension, as Clarke (1996: 56) observes, was worth only a quarter of the wage of a labourer; that married couples were paid at a lower rate; and that anyone on poor relief was initially ineligible for a pension (this despite the fact that aged paupers were most in need of one). The terms of the construction of old age is clear: a minimum level of provision but with maximum expectation that this would be seen as sufficient reward by the recipients.[1]

This initial approach to regulating old age was largely successful in its attempt to limit the numbers of people who were both old and dependent on public support (as opposed to being old and employed). This aspect was brought out in the debate on the Old Age Pensions Bill in 1908. Lloyd George, answering suggestions that the age limit should be 65 instead of 70, argued that:

> The expenditure would be too great to begin with and in my own judgement I do not think that it is the best way of dealing with the period between 65 and 70. I am not sure that the German method is not the best here. It deals with infirmity rather than age. That is the test under 70. I can well understand a man of 70 saying, 'I am willing to retire, I have earned my pension'. There are many men of 65, 66 and 67 who are much more effective and vigorous and capable of doing good work than many men of 57. I think when we come to deal, as I hope we will in the near future, with the problem of infirmity, that will be the time to consider the question of the broken down old man of 67 and 68 who is left to charity. (*Hansard*, 1908, vol. 190, col. 575)

In the period when Lloyd George was speaking, 606 out of every 1,000 men over the age of 65 were still working. Hence his argument had a strong foundation in the existing pattern of employment. But the use of the term 'broken down old man' is revealing. True, its accuracy for elderly men, after a lifetime of labour in a harsh industrial and social environment, often with poor standards of nutrition, cannot be underestimated (Stearns, 1975). But the fact that the problem is put just in terms of men is significant, ignoring the point that it was women who were living longest, and who were most likely to experience directly old age (as their numbers in workhouses graphically illustrated). And the term 'broken down' itself is important, reflecting as it does a historical tradition of identifying the retired working-class elderly as useless, worn-out and unemployable – to be grouped with the infirm and feeble-minded as a category in social policy. The possibility or the potential being experienced some other way is hardly countenanced, for if the elderly are not ready to be included among the infirm and the feeble-minded, then it is work which is put forward as the obvious alternative. Seemingly, there is nothing in between.

The limits to state involvement in supporting the elderly were again brought out in the second reading of the Conservative's Contributory Pensions Bill in 1925. The Bill provided for a pension of 10 shillings a week, which the minister (Neville Chamberlain) moving the Bill admitted was: 'obviously insufficient by itself to provide a grown man or woman with the necessities for life'. Two reasons were cited for this. The first was financial, that a larger pension would inflict an excessive burden both on industry and the state. The second was that fixing the pensions at such a level would encourage the virtue of thrift. According to Chamberlain:

> We believe that there are many people who today feel that it is perfectly hopeless for them to try and provide completely for their needs in old age, but that when they see this scheme they feel they have a foundation upon which it is worth their while to try and build on something more. In that way we shall be encouraging those virtues of thrift which have done so much for the country in the past. (*Hansard*, 1924, vol. 184, col. 79)

The main consequence of this policy was that it still became necessary for many to continue to work after the age of 65 – particularly in the absence of any savings. It also confirmed that for those who were unable to continue to work, and who had little or no savings, poverty became the automatic consequence of retirement and old age.

The US experience bears similarities to the above. Quadagno notes that by 1937, 40 states had pension plans approved by the Social Security Board (set up after the 1935 Social Security Act). Many of the plans had eligibility requirements reflecting poor law philosophy. She reports that 25 states required an investigation to determine the ability of other members of the family to support the applicant. These 25 plans variously specified that the applicant could not have 'children' or 'relatives legally responsible', or in some cases 'persons legally responsible', who were able to provide support. There were also variations in property and income limitations in terms of the maximum or minimum allowed. Quadagno concludes from this that:

> . . . the strong values of voluntarism and thrift served as an impediment to developing an old age pension system that was free from the stigma of relief. When a national pension plan was enacted, it reflected our society's ambivalence about redistributing income without incorporating some test of need. The Social Security Act was a complex picture of nearly every social welfare device known and included poor law criteria for eligibility in its old age assistance title. (1986: 150)

Reconstructing old age: 1940–1990

The argument developed above is that old age – up until the mid-twentieth century – was contained within a narrow phase of the life course, one which was heavily circumscribed by the likelihood of poverty and an early death. From the 1940s, however, as reviewed in Chapter 3, a process of reconstruction took place, beginning, first, with the establishment of the welfare state; second, with the emergence of retirement as a distinctive and valued part of life (Maddox, 1966; Phillipson, 1978). These developments helped to open out a new stage in the life course, one which seemed to suggest greater optimism about the nature of older age as a social relationship. Katz argues here that: 'Pension and retirement programs played their part in constituting the modern life course' (1996: 60). Similarly, Cole spells out the importance of these two elements as follows:

> In linking retirement benefits to a specific age, public pension systems provided the economic basis for a chronologically defined phase of life beyond gainful employment. By the mid-twentieth century, this 'new' phase of life was becoming a mass phenomenon. Increasing life expectancy, the dramatic growth of the elderly population, the spread of retirement and the expansion of Social Security benefits transformed old age into the final stage of the institutionalized life cycle. (1992: 223)

However, there are differing interpretations about the construction of old age in this period. Cole, for example, emphasizes the way in which the opening out of old age actually led to a new type of marginalization:

> Between the 1920s and the 1960s, the reconstruction of old age (which became the capstone of the institutionalized lifecourse) proceeded on the assumption that most old people cannot contribute significantly to the 'real world' (i.e. the labour market). Social policy often defined the elderly as clients or patients in need of professional expertise and intervention. As Social Security benefits became more generous, older people retreated or were moved to the margins of society. (1992: 232–3)

Yet it may be more plausible to develop other assessments of this period. In the first place, retirement seemed to be developing as a period with its own validity and potential for new lifestyles (Biggs, 1993). Inequality within retirement was, and remains, a major concern (Phillipson, 1994). But the argument was also being made (notably by activists such as Maggie Kuhn) that marginality through enforced retirement could be resisted; that older people could develop a new type of engagement which offered a challenge to mainstream society. Second, the apparent generosity of welfare reforms referred to by Cole (a view perhaps overstated for Britain and the USA) misses the point about the essential objectives of the welfare state. Here, the foundation of the post-war welfare state was tied to a broader conception of citizenship, and the social incorporation of groups hitherto excluded through the operation of the Poor Law.

In the case of Britain, Peter Hennessy (1993) sees the welfare state as '*the* talisman of a better postwar [society]'. For Marshall (1949), the welfare state added a third dimension to the historical evolution of citizenship (following on from civil and political rights), with social rights in the form of pensions, health and education. That the level of benefits remained undeniably low (as already noted in Chapter 5) is important to stress. But the idea of social inclusion was fundamental. In the case of the Beveridge Plan, this was seen to be: '. . . not a system for the poor only but for the whole of society' (Bartley et al., 1997). Older people had become 'citizens', assured of a minimum amount of income which aimed to achieve a decent level of subsistence (Myles, 1996). As Timmins notes, this reflected the aim of the welfare state in 'shifting resources between generations at key moments in life'. He summarizes this as follows:

> People paid in taxes in middle life when in work, and in return were helped with their children's upbringing and education, were guaranteed help when sick, and were assisted in old age when earnings ceased. There was therefore and remained a widespread vested interest – or, to put it more kindly, a mutual interest – in the welfare state, on top of the 'never again' revulsion felt over the effects of the 1930s depression. (1996: 163)

The 'dualism' of retirement on the one side, and the welfare state on the other, in fact offered rather more than the marginalization referred to by Cole. From a historical perspective, for example, we can see that both elements provided the basis for a new and somewhat novel vision of the relationship between society and older age. In the earlier period, old age was constructed around notions of dependency built around surviving elements of the Poor Law. In this second period, the space within which old age was constructed was enlarged and redefined. Elements of the Poor Law unquestionably remained but the scope of intervention was massively extended. Indeed, some commentators expressed caution about the new, expanded vocabulary of ageing. Richard Cottam, for example, in a contribution to a collection of papers published in the early 1950s on the topic of living longer, argued:

> The new interest which society is showing in older people has not been entirely to their advantage; indeed, they have suffered not a little from the floodlight which the post-war years have turned on them. 'The Aged', 'Old People', 'the elderly infirm', 'the frail ambulant', 'the Eventide of Life', are terms now in common use and the new titles . . . are in danger of turning what

is a perfectly normal group of people in every community in every civilisation into a specially classified group. (1954: 7)

In part, this categorization was the price for eroding the distinction between the 'deserving' and 'undeserving' old. However, it also reflected the fact that, despite an initial flurry of concern in the late 1940s and early 1950s, there was broad acceptance of the need to treat older people as a special group existing outside the labour market (Graebner, 1980; Phillipson, 1982). It is now possible to see, in fact, that the new unitary category of old age was a substantial advance over the earlier period. It was quickly seized upon, as noted in Chapter 2, as the natural constituency of an expanding layer of medical and social welfare professionals. This, despite the undoubted problems and contradictions noted by researchers such as Estes (1979; 1993), clearly positioned older people as a core group within the welfare state. Indeed, there appeared to be a general political consensus, at least up until the mid-1970s, that increasing the welfare budget (through general taxation) for the elderly, was a central responsibility of modern government.

The identity of the old was, then, influenced by, in Taylor's (see Chapter 4) terms, a moral framework which developed through the welfare state. This, in fact, provided a language and set of images for shaping the identity of older people. Increasingly, however, in this period (and especially in the 1960s and 1970s), the 'welfare self' in old age existed alongside another important element – namely the evolution of the idea of an 'active retirement'. It is important here to appreciate the way in which the notion of retirement as something 'positive' took time to spread beyond relatively small groups of retirees. For working-class people, retirement was traditionally associated with exhaustion and an early death – hence the cynicism expressed by many about pension plans. However, the 'need' for retirement was also clear. As Stearns puts it: '. . . workers wanted to retire. Their whole culture and experience taught them that work deteriorated rapidly after a certain age' (1975: 261).

Initially, in the early post-war period, the focus was on the idea of retirement as a social-psychological crisis, with the likelihood of increased morbidity and mortality being cited in the research literature (Phillipson, 1993). As argued in Chapter 5, this was seen as a consequence of the loss of work-based friendships, and the reduction in status and self-esteem associated with old age. By the 1960s and 1970s, however, a new generation of studies was providing a more positive view of retirement. The potential for it to be experienced as a major stage in the life course was emphasized in this period, with the development of more active lifestyles being fostered in what was increasingly referred to as the 'third age' (Young and Schuller, 1991; Bernard and Meade, 1993). Research now acknowledged the crucial role of income in terms of its influence on the retirement experience. Atchley (1976; 1982), for example, conducted a series of studies in the USA through the late 1960s and 1970s, all of which pointed to the impact of reduced income, and the change in lifestyle associated with it, as the major factor in producing negative retirement attitudes. From his research, Atchley found little evidence for those with moderate incomes and above actually 'missing work' to any great extent.

Palmore et al.'s (1985) analysis of a number of US longitudinal data sets concluded that:

1 Retirement at the normal age has little or no adverse effects on health for the average retiree. Some have health declines, but these are balanced by those who enjoy health improvement.
2 Retirement at the normal age has few substantial effects on activities, except for the obvious reduction in work and some compensating increase in solitary activities.
3 Retirement at the normal age has little or no effect on most attitudes for the average retiree. Some become more dissatisfied, but these are balanced by those who become more satisfied (Palmore et al., 1985: 167; see also Phillipson, 1993).

This research, it should be noted, was conducted before the rapid falls in labour force participation of the 1980s, and was based upon interviews with cohorts of men and women who had managed to work up to (or beyond) either the minimum or maximum age limit for their occupation. Research on retirement also tended to emphasize the problems facing men, the difficulties confronting women being largely ignored in geron-tological literature at least up until the 1980s (Stone and Minkler, 1984; Arber and Ginn, 1991).

None the less, the idea of constructing an identity within retirement was increasingly emphasized both in the research literature and within society at large. This was also linked to perspectives which focused on the retired (and the early retired in particular) developing new patterns of consumption, notably within areas such as education and leisure. This point was raised by Featherstone where he examined the way in which middle age was being redefined as a more youthful phase of life, one which also extended into retirement:

> Pre-retirement planning today is presented as the management of life-style and consumption opportunities to enable retirement to be a progressive set of options and choices – a phase in which the individual is presented as still moving within the social space, still learning, investing in cultural capital and putting off the inevitable disengagement of deep old age. (1987: 134)

Considerable evidence emerged for the phenomenon described by Featherstone, with a substantial section of the service sector recognizing the importance of the 50 plus market for their future growth. The obvious examples here would be the specialist retirement magazines, holiday companies, retirement communities and private sheltered housing schemes. These were the outward trappings of a significant group within the older population, one concerned to develop a positive lifestyle in the years following departure from paid employment.

The potential of older people to re-engage within the cultural and educational sphere was examined in some detail by Peter Laslett (1989) in his book *A Fresh Map of Life*. Laslett's study was a manifesto for older people in Britain, urging them to exploit the benefits of demographic change. Thus, he noted that the male expectation of life in Britain implies that a man leaving work at the age of 55 can look forward to spending as much time in retirement as he will spend in employment after reaching his mid-30s, 20 more years at his job and 20 years after he has left it. The corresponding figures for women are even more striking given that they live longer and have, historically, retired ahead of men. Laslett (1989) viewed this in the context of a transformation in the use of free time, which had moved from the province of an elite to a commodity possessed by millions of elderly citizens. He presented the case for older people re-engaging in the cultural sphere, becoming the standard-bearers for values likely to be neglected in the second age (the period of earning and saving).

From the above perspective, therefore, there was the prospect of reconstructing identity within the third age. On the one hand, older people could adopt lifestyles built around new patterns of consumption. On the other hand, there was a broader notion of the retired entering a period of greater personal fulfilment, with engagement in educational and cultural activities becoming an important aspect of their lives.

This vision of retirement was important, then, in expanding the idea of what constitutes an older person. Increasingly, retirement was viewed not as an impediment to good mental health (a widespread view in the 1950s); rather, it was seen as a viable pathway to a level of fulfilment unlikely to be achieved within the workplace. This view rested, however, to a very large extent on acceptance of high levels of retirement in general and early retirement in particular. As discussed in Chapter Four, the conditions for this were encouraging for almost two decades – from the late 1960s to the late 1980s – given the need to restructure industry and adapt to new technologies. In contrast, retirement was to be seen as somewhat more marginal given the anxieties of the 1990s, where high levels of unemployment now coexisted with concern about the ability of economies to support its dependent populations. This shift in the positioning of retirement, while not erasing entirely the idea of a positive third age and related notions, did produce tensions in the social relationship between older retirees and society. The implications of this development will now be reviewed.

Rights and risk in old age

The argument of the preceding section was that old age was recon-structed after the Second World War, first on the basis of social rights associated with pensions and related benefits; second (but more gradu-ally), the idea of the right to an extended period of retirement. A third important theme (as identified in Chapter 7) was the notion of an intergenerational contract, with the young and middle aged supporting elderly citizens – partly on a reciprocal basis given their contribution to work and welfare earlier in their life; partly with the expectation on the part of younger generations that they would receive similar assistance when they were old.

These developments peaked in certain crucial respects during the 1970s.[2] In the case of both Britain and the USA, pension reform, to take the clearest example, seemed at last to be making headway. The British case has already been summarized, with the rising value of the basic state pension coming alongside legislation for a second tier of pensions (in the form of SERPS). For a brief period in Britain, there seemed to be cross-party consensus over the issue of pensions. Indeed, Ellis, writing of the period immediately following the passing of the legislation on SERPS, notes that: 'for the first time in twenty years pensions and their future were off the political agenda' (cited in Timmins, 1996: 350).

In the USA, Quadagno (1996: 400) notes that with Democrats and Republicans courting older people for their votes in an election year, the 1972 Congress agreed a substantial rise in Social Security benefits. These were increased by as much as 20 per cent, with, of even greater importance, benefits indexed to future inflation. Quadagno views the 1972 amendments as representing a turning point for Social Security: 'the automatic cost-of-living increases removed benefits from politics and ensured older people that inflation would not erode the value of benefits' (1996: 400). Quadagno summarizes the implications as follows:

> By the mid-1970s more than 80 per cent of those over age 65 were receiving some income from Social Security. Social Security also helped widows and widowers with dependent children and provided income security for the disabled. Social Security was one of the few government programmes where people received something tangible for their taxes, and as a result public support for Social Security was high. Virtually every public opinion poll between 1977 and 1983 indicated that US citizens supported Social Security. The 1972 amendments had solidly incorporated the middle class into the welfare state. (1996: 400)

Notwithstanding such support, the 1980s saw the progressive erosion of key elements in the older people's welfare state. In the case of Britain, Walker (1995), for example, notes that in contrast to expansionist plans for welfare reform in the 1960s and 1970s, the focus in subsequent years was almost exclusively on plans to residualize the basic state pension, target resources on the poorest, and privatize the provision of second-tier pensions. As part of the general onslaught on public spending, Walker suggests that: '. . . the spectre of the economic burden of old age was used more and more openly to justify restraint in, first, social security expenditures and, subsequently, health and social services spending' (1995: 26).

Indeed, it is of some significance that while expenditure on the welfare state continued to grow in the Thatcher and post-Thatcher years, its scope was substantially reduced in relation to older people. Timmins, for example, suggests that pensions 'became the one large part of the welfare state where [governments] did succeed in rolling back the frontiers' (1996: 403). And in the case of health and social care, reforms in the field of community care produced extensive cuts and rationalization in services targeted at older people (Phillipson, 1994). On the one hand, in the case of the National Health Service, the period from the mid-1970s to the mid-1990s saw a substantial reduction in convalescent and con- tinuing care facilities for older people. Over the period 1976 to 1994, the number of NHS beds specifically for older people fell from 55,600 to 37,500, a 33 per cent reduction (House of Commons, 1995). This trend was further reinforced by the fall in the number of acute beds (24 per cent in the period 1982 to 1993/4), this having its biggest impact on elderly people who accounted for nearly half (47 per cent) of all acute bed days in 1992/3 (Department of Health, 1994).

At the same time, despite the retreat of the institutional sector, the supply of domiciliary services fell behind the growth of the older population. Over the period 1986/7 to 1992/3, the number of home helps and meals on wheels fell 10 and 13 per cent respectively per head of population aged 75 and over (House of Commons Health Committee, 1994). Other community services, such as domiciliary nursing, also fell behind the expansion of the very elderly population. Between 1983/4 and 1993/4, the number of full-time equivalent district nursing staff grew by just 7.5 per cent, with the number of district nursing contacts falling from 2.4 million in 1988/9 to 2.1 million in 1992/3 (DoH and OPCS, 1995).

Evidence for the crisis in the field of community care, has been the subject of extensive research in the USA in various studies led by Carroll Estes (Estes, 1986; Estes et al., 1993). Her research has documented the crisis in care arising from the privatization of profitable services; the impact of bureaucratization (industry consolidation and rationalization); service fragmentation; and deepening class divisions in access. These trends are reinforced (as in Britain) by the contracting out of services once undertaken directly by government. Here, Estes and Linkins (1997) refer to the concept of the 'hollow state' to describe the separation between government and the services it funds. Such a state routinely contracts out its production capability to third parties, reserving for itself responsibilities attached to monitoring and inspection.

Changes in funding have run alongside the restructuring of health and social care. In the context of the USA, there is the emergence of a more deeply stratified system of *de facto* rationing based on ability to pay (Estes et al., 1996). In Britain, there is a clear expectation on the part of government that private spending will assume an increasingly important role in health-care expenditure. Over the 15 years to 1993, such spending grew in fact from 5 to 10 per cent of overall expenditure on health. Summarizing the implications of this development, Andrew Dilnot argues as follows:

> All of the forces that led to the shift to private provision in pensions are present. And with every marginal increase in the role of private as opposed to public provision, the scope for shifting back to universal public provision is reduced. Looking ahead, there seems every likelihood that in the next decade, on current policies, the share of private spending will double again in [areas such as] health . . . And it is important to note that some evidence suggests, unsurprisingly perhaps, that private consumption of health care reduces support for enhanced tax funded public provision, so that there is the risk that shifting the better off out of public provision may reduce the support for public spending rather than simply reduce demands on the public system. (1997: 1–2)

This transformation in fact reflects a more general shift from the public provision characteristic of what Lash and Urry refer to as 'organized capitalism', to the more flexible arrangements running through the period of 'disorganized capitalism' (see Chapter 4). This development has served to change once again the definition of what it means to be an older person. In the conditions of advanced modernity, growing old moves from being a collective to an individual experience. The notion of an ageing society (with social responsibilities) becomes secondary to the emphasis on ageing individuals – with the crisis of ageing seen to originate in how individuals rather than societies handle the demands associated with social ageing.

These developments have transformed the institutional space occupied by older people. For much of the post-war period this was dominated by externalities of different kinds: of which welfare, retirement and kinship were the most important. The discourses associated with these institutions were fundamental in shaping subjectivity within older age. The subject status of the older person was reproduced through a combination of identities, these reflecting the interplay of the 'retired self', the 'welfare self', and the 'family' or 'kinship self'. Crucially, these identities had begun to develop some kind of legitimation for older age. At the beginning of this period, of course, this was still built on relatively fragile foundations. Peter Townsend's (1957) moving account of the experience of retired men in Bethnal Green illustrates the way in which, as late as the mid-twentieth century, retirement was still open to resistance within working-class culture. Moreover, as critics such as Gouldner (1971) and Estes (1979; 1993) were to point out, the welfare state was itself hardly benign in the way it treated and processed groups such as older persons.

However, it is important to emphasize what Titmuss and others have referred to as the 'moral purpose of the welfare state'. Rodney Lowe (1993), for example, argues that its defenders saw its role going far beyond that of relief of a hard core of deprivation. The first concern was to provide social justice in the form of compensation for the social costs of economic change. A second concern, however, was to highlight the role of welfare in moving society on to a higher ethical ground. Lowe suggests that the welfare state was seen as being able to 'elevate society by institutionalizing a deeper sense of community and mutual care' (1993: 21).

Older people were central, in fact, to this idea of the welfare state as embodying a sense of 'moral progress' (Leonard, 1997: 21). People saw care for the old both as a fair exchange for past work and services (for example, in times of war), and as an indication that society had moved on from treating old age merely as one of the many risks in life. In the 1990s, however, this particular vision about the status of old age has become somewhat clouded. We seem to be rather less sure about how we justify the status of being 'retired', or being 'dependent on the welfare state', or 'needing one's family' to provide support. Are these legitimate statuses and requirements? Can they be justified given financial and demographic constraints? Such concerns are now caught up in wider anxieties about what is viewed as an 'inequitable' welfare state (see Chapter 7). Here perhaps, one might argue, has been the biggest failure of the post-war period in relation to older people. At the birth of the welfare state, the old were being singled out as expensive 'passengers'; more than half a century on, they have become the 'drones', feeding off the more productive activities of others. This, in many respects, constitutes the real crisis of welfare in the post-war period: namely, that the redefinition of old age could never quite escape the idea of the old as a 'burden', a creation of the twentieth century but one which, as the century draws to an end, has yet to find a clear place or purpose to carry forward to the next. In the penultimate chapter of this book, we examine some ideas for developing and reshaping the status and identity of older people.

Notes

1 Timmins notes that the pensions were dubbed by their grateful recipients 'the Lord George', on the grounds that 'only a Lord could afford to be so generous'. Timmins (1996: 13) writes: 'The pensions, Lloyd George declared, lifted "The shadow of the workhouse from the homes of the poor". Churchill, more temperately, declared of the first relatively meagre means-tested payments: "We have not pretended to carry the toiler on to dry land. What we have done is to strap a lifebelt about him".'

2 See Lowe (1993) for a detailed assessment of this trend.

9

RECONSTRUCTING OLD AGE: POLICY OPTIONS

If the twentieth century redrew the shape of the life course, the tasks in the next century will be to develop a greater measure of security and validity for this period in life. In attempting this, it is increasingly clear that the term 'old age' (used somewhat uncritically throughout this book) is almost certainly unsatisfactory. Evidence of this can be seen in a number of ways, but two are of particular importance. First, it is now apparent (as was argued in the previous chapter), that the label 'older person' has diminished rather than enhanced the lives of those to whom it is applied. This is the rather grim conclusion one is forced to draw from the history of provision for people defined as old, with the welfare state actually contributing rather less to the status of older people than its founders might reasonably have hoped. Second, and of greater long-term importance, is the changing composition of the groups and individuals making up the third and fourth age. These have been summarized by Conrad in the following way:

> The socio-economic discrepancies inside this population are no less formidable than in the younger age groups: between the 55-year-old steel worker who is half unemployed and half early retired and the 70-year-old policy consultant on a second career, between 'new old' middle-class wives and widows on culture trips and the permanent hotel dwellers, between senior golf champs and the victims of work disability, chronic diseases, and dementia there are probably immense and probably increasing inequalities. These contrasts make it doubtful whether the term 'old age' can still serve as a conceptual roof for all these situations. (1992: 65)

Both these arguments underline the case for rethinking the framework defining older age. Moreover, the case is reinforced given the questioning of the legitimacy of the claim of the elderly to a fair share of resources, in particular through access to a state pension rising in line with the nation's prosperity. The apparent political consensus that this is 'unaffordable' has raised fundamental issues about the future facing older people. This issue now needs tackling with the utmost urgency if the lives of a substantial number of pensioners are not to be blighted by insecurity and anxiety about the future.

One suggestion to be developed here is that, in the context of a new century, we begin to move away from the limitations now associated with the nomenclature associated with growing old. We need, it is suggested, an approach that can give legitimacy to the variety of experiences which people are likely to have in the second half of life. The crisis of ageing at the present time is that there appears to be no social mechanism for recognizing the range of contributions made by people over the whole of the life course. Calling people 'old' seems, on the one hand, to foreclose wider debate; on the other, to drastically limit future options. 'Older people' are now faced with a crisis of invisibility urgently demanding a response both from themselves as well as from political and cultural institutions. In this chapter we examine some core policy options, outlining these as a contribution to what promises to be a major debate for the twenty-first century.

Emancipation from traditional ageing

A starting point is to stress the possibility of emancipating people from conventional or traditional approaches to ageing. As argued at various points in this study, these have been directly associated with particular discourses associated with the welfare state on the one hand, and retirement on the other. However, the changes to these institutions clearly offer possibilities for older people to reposition their own identities, and to redefine the scope of ageing as a social and personal event.

The argument here is that we are seeing a shift from an ageing characteristic of the early and middle phases of modernity, to one associated with 'late modernity'. The key element is the reconstruction of later life as a period of potential choice on the one hand; but also of risk and danger on the other. This tension has arguably been present throughout the twentieth century. However, as is argued below, in the twenty-first century it will be fundamental to the way in which growing old is experienced with, of course, far greater numbers of people actually involved.

A starting point for understanding this is what Giddens (1991) calls the 'crisis-prone nature of late modernity'. This, Giddens suggests, has unsettling consequences in at least two respects: 'it fuels a general climate of uncertainty which an individual finds disturbing no matter how far he seeks to put it to the back of his mind; and it inevitably exposes everyone to a diversity of crisis situations of greater or lesser importance, crisis situations that may threaten the very core of identity' (1991: 184–5). One response to this has been for individuals to separate themselves, in their day-to-day life, from those events which provoke deep-seated anxieties. Giddens defines this as the 'sequestration of experience' and he summarizes its main features as follows:

> Existential questions and doubts raise some of the most basic anxieties human beings can face. By and large, under conditions of modernity, such questions do not have to be confronted directly; they are institutionally 'put aside' rather than handled within the personality of the individual. So far as the control of anxiety is concerned, this situation has paradoxical implications. On the one hand, in ordinary circumstances, the individual is relatively protected from issues which might otherwise pose themselves as disturbing questions. On the other hand, whenever fateful moments intervene or other kinds of personal crises occur, the sense of ontological security is likely to come under immediate strain. (1991: 185)

In relation to ageing, the suggestion that might be made is that the institutions of retirement and the welfare state played an important role in bracketing out many fundamental anxieties associated with events such as the loss of work in early older age, to loss of bodily function in late older age. These are without question major anxieties; indeed, it might be argued that they have come to represent some of our most fundamental concerns. People do without question fear what Featherstone and Hepworth (1989) term 'bodily betrayals'; they are certainly anxious about what happens to them after the ending of paid employment.

The difference now, however, is that it is less easy to 'bracket out' or to 'sequester' these anxieties. Decisions, for example, about coping with particular forms of dependency are now individual decisions (part of the new politics of consumerism). The choices may indeed be limited, but increasingly they are thrust upon individuals and/or their informal carers. With the reconstruction of the welfare state (with, for example, the increasing reliance upon residential home care), people are forced into making difficult choices and trade offs in relation to questions such as the financing of their personal care in old age; where this takes place; and the nature of the person providing the service. Again, in relation to retirement as a whole, the scope for decision-making has been drastically widened. Increasingly, people are being called upon to build retirement around their own individual planning, both in relation to finances and the timing and manner in which they leave the workplace. These questions indicate that older age has simultaneously become a major source of 'risk' but also a potential source of 'liberation'. Old age does threaten disaster – poverty, severe illness, the loss of a loved one. But it also can bring the opposite: freedom from restrictive work and domestic roles; new relationships; and a greater feeling of security. People do truly ride a 'juggernaut' in older age, and this is making the period more rather than less central as an issue of concern for social and economic policy.

As this suggests, there is a wider set of issues here which means that decisions about growing old cannot just be left to individuals or their families. The tension is between growing old as a collective or social experience, and the process as internalized and 'given voice' by individuals. The underlying concern of this study has been with the contradictions and conflicts between these levels. As discussed in Chapter 4, what brings these two sides together is the nature of identity in old age. One view of this might be that people actually arrive in old age with a secure identity (and life story) to hand, one that (barring particular mental health problems) will sustain the individual through most of the difficult passages or transitions encountered in old age. This has been one of the most popular (and arguably most damaging) stereotypes about older people: namely, that for them at least identity work is largely complete. Indeed, identity is seen to become all pervasive as the body gradually disintegrates around them.

But let us read identity in a different way, drawing on the work of Giddens and Taylor as discussed earlier in this book. Giddens (1991), for example, rejects the view of the self as a stable entity persisting unchanged over time. On the contrary, he argues: 'Self-identity . . . is not something that is just given, as a result of the individual's action system, but something that has to be routinely created and sustained in the reflexive activities of the individual' (1991: 52). And Giddens goes on to make what is perhaps a seminal point in relation to the self in old age:

> The existential nature of self-identity is bound up with the fragile nature of the biography which the individual 'supplies' about herself. A person's identity is not to be found in behaviour, nor – important though this is – in the reaction of others, but in the capacity *to keep a particular narrative going*. The individual's biography, if she is to maintain regular interaction with others in the day-to-day world, cannot be wholly fictive. It must continually integrate events which occur in the external world, and sort them into the ongoing 'story' about the self. As Charles Taylor puts it, 'In order to have a sense of who we are, we have to have a notion of how we have become, and of where we are going'. (1991: 54)

These arguments have immense implications for our understanding of some of the issues facing older people, allowing us to see more clearly the disjunction that has opened up between the world as routinely experienced by older people, and their own self-identity. The story of the self in old age now seems somewhat unclear: neither a 'welfare state self' nor a 'retirement self' seem wholly acceptable. In the economic uncertainties of late capitalism, older age has become somewhat tarnished as a social good. But in Taylor's terms this raises rather acutely the issue of where older people are going. What is there beyond retirement and the welfare state? What are the moral resources that older people are to draw upon if the institutions associated with welfare and the inter-generational contract are placed in doubt?

Pensions and welfare

Our response to these questions should not be to privilege one particular side in the debate. In this sense, I am not arguing in favour of a simple return to some pre-Thatcherite social policy. An evolving welfare state and institution of retirement was beginning to provide a framework for older age, but the debate has clearly moved on and other options must be considered. Nor am I arguing for a narrow 'postmodern' view of ageing which focuses simply on choice and reflexivity, ignoring the profound inequalities of class, gender and ethnicity which continue to shape the lives of older people. In fact, I wish to draw a middle position between these two: arguing, first, for a framework which provides the necessary financial support for older people; but, second, for greater flexibility as regards the way in which older age is allowed to develop within society.

In the case of the former, this means urgent attention to particular areas within social policy. In Britain, the most important of these concerns the state pension. The spiralling decline in its value – likely to be just 9 per cent of average earnings by the year 2000 – is posing fundamental issues both for current and future cohorts of older people. The state pension remains the most sensible and realistic option for providing a basic income for older age. To put some perspective on schemes to encourage additional 'stakeholder pensions', almost 60 per cent of the adult population in Britain are not in a position to save on a regular basis. Among this group – the majority of the working popula-tion – are the unemployed, those in low-paying or insecure jobs, and the economically inactive. For this group, increasing the value of the state pension is the only effective route to a secure retirement.

Establishing the framework for additional pensions remains import-ant, but is less significant than the task of rescuing the state retirement pension: this must be a central goal for social policy for older people as we move into the twenty-first century. In a broader context, the case for restoring the value of the pension must also be linked with the kind of future we want to have for older age. Here, it is important to remind ourselves that the state pension has never been linked to a realistic standard of living for older people, one that would allow their full participation within society. The consequence of this is that the majority of older people have always been forced into reliance upon means-tested benefits, or (as around 900,000 have done consistently in the post-war period) simply not claimed benefits which they are fully entitled to receive.

This brings out the point that restoring the value of the state pension is actually as much an issue about the kind of old age we want to develop as a straightforward financial issue (a point highlighted in more detail in Chapter 5). This point can be made both in a narrow sense in terms of what we choose to spend our money on, as well as in a wider sense concerning the values which we want to prioritize. On the former, it might be noted that the additional gross cost of increasing the state pension in line with earnings, assuming that these increase by 1.75 per cent more than prices, would be £1,320 million in 1999–2000 (1.75 is mid-way between the 1.5 per cent and 2 per cent used in official projections). The net cost would be far less, because one in three pensioners would pay tax on the increase (National Pensioner Convention, 1998). One thousand, three hundred and twenty million pounds sounds a substantial sum of money, but should be compared with the £17 billion spent in a 10-year period from the mid-1980s on the promotion of personal pensions. This money (which represents the charges imposed for administering schemes) actually represents a net loss to taxpayers as it is certainly more than they will save through reduced spending on state pensions.

In any event, the reality of the situation in Britain is that expenditure on social security is substantially less than in most other European countries. Taking together all spending – state and private – on old age, sickness, unemployment and disability, Britain spends less than £3,000 a head annually, France around £5,000 and Denmark almost £7,000 (*Social Trends*, 1998). Moreover, spending on the elderly in particular is well below international trends. OECD figures for 1993 show the UK to spend 5.88 per cent of GDP expenditure on old-age benefits, compared with 7.53 per cent for the Netherlands, 7.26 per cent for Germany, 9.47 per cent for Sweden, and 9.73 per cent for France (Adonis, 1998). Only four OECD countries spend less than Britain: Ireland, Portugal, the USA and Japan.

But, as already indicated, there are wider issues that must also be noted. Limiting expenditure on the old, and in particular eroding the value of the state pension, also sends out a particular message about where responsibility for financial support really lies. Reducing the state pension to a derisory or 'nugatory' amount conveys a particular view about society's commitment to older people. Pensions increasingly seem to be regarded more as a sectional than a societal interest. People are seen to earn pensions as 'employees' rather than 'citizens'; pensions have become as much a 'personal' undertaking as a 'social' right. The shift in language here is striking, and almost certainly damaging to the interests both of older people now and indeed of future generations. Placing responsibility for pensions back as an issue for all generations – as a collective responsibility – is central to restoring the basis for a viable identity for elderly people in the years ahead.

This argument is especially relevant given the changes within paid employment identified in Chapter 5. The implication here was that continuous employment, as a basis for securing financial provision for old age, has been steadily undermined over the last two decades. The corollary of this is that increasing inequalities are likely to arise from taking the traditional male pattern of work as typical of workers now (and of women in particular) and using it as a basis for organizing pensions and other benefits in the future.

The problem – for some men and virtually all women – is how to secure financial coverage in the context of demographic change and the reorganization of the life course. For many women there is a form of 'triple jeopardy' arising from these developments. First, the growth of a flexible workforce has been especially strong among women and has led to significant forms of discrimination in respect of wages and career development (Hewitt, 1993; Itzin and Phillipson, 1993). Second, rights to employment have been significantly affected by women's role as carers. A study of non-spouse carers by Glendinning (1992) found that a quarter of the carers interviewed had had to give up paid work altogether; most had already had to change jobs, reduce their hours of work or lose earnings for other reasons before finishing work completely. Third, low rates of pay have translated into deprivation in terms of limited access to pensions along with high levels of poverty in late old age (Ginn and Arber, 1995).

In the case of both men and women who leave employment ahead of state retirement age, the likelihood is that they will enter a financially insecure pathway in the transition from work to retirement. Kohli and Rein (1991) make the important point that pathways invariably make use of institutional arrangements that were originally constructed for purposes other than early exit – usually to cover specific risks that were thought to be the exception rather than the rule (such as unemployment or disability). They conclude that: 'Incorporating them into pathways of early exit means that they are now used to deal not with specific risks but with the burden of a whole age group. The old instruments came to be transformed into new tools for labour market regulation' (Kohli and Rein, 1991: 13).

In policy terms, the above trends suggest major changes are needed in the design of pensions and the support for workers when unemployed. In particular, the pension system of the future will need to be one which is detached from assumptions about continuous participation in paid work. Instead, such benefits should be attached to individual citizenship rights, reflecting the diversity of socially useful roles in which individuals engage throughout their lives (Bornat et al., 1985; Waerness, 1989). The basis for such a system must be acknowledgement of the growth of different types of paid employment alongside greater flexibility in terms of the organization of working life.

A number of implications follow from these arguments: first, social security in the future will need to be based on a view of productive activities taking place in a range of locations, outside as well as inside the marketplace. This will entail giving equal value to both care work and waged work, ensuring that those who on a full- or part-time basis care for the old or the young do not suffer financial penalties in their own old age.

Second, social security will need to operate with a different view of the life course, one in which paid work is concentrated into a limited period of years, but where different forms of flexible working in terms of the entry and exit into work become more common. The issue for the future is how to ensure that flexibility within the occupational system does not translate into disadvantage in respect of benefits and financial provision for old age. Preventing this in fact strengthens the case for an insurance-based system of financial support. The idea of 'pooling risks' has, in fact, become more rather than less important given earlier retirement and increased insecurity within the workplace.

Third, more immediate reforms are needed to protect the position of older workers who are caught between the end of employment and receipt of a state pension (Laczko and Phillipson, 1991). One realistic possibility might be rights to indefinite unemployment benefit for men and women who have spent a specific number years in the labour force and/or care work within the home (see Brown, 1990, for one illustration of this point).

Fourth, reforms will also be needed to provide greater security in employment for older workers and mature women workers. The key to such a policy is to treat older workers as a human resource which can provide considerable benefits to an employing organization (O'Reilly and Caro, 1994; OECD, 1998). This means giving older workers and mature women workers full access to retraining, job redesign, staff development schemes, and related facilities (Itzin and Phillipson, 1993). At present, because of the combined effect of age discrimination at work and high levels of unemployment, older workers are treated as a marginal and disposable element within the workforce. This increases the likelihood of them experiencing forced early exit with the potential financial penalty of an impoverished old age (Laczko, 1990).

Fifth, the developments reviewed in this chapter reflect changes in the meanings associated with periods in the life course, as well as trans-formations in economic and social relationships. The need to change the way pensions are provided is not simply because establishing eligibility through employment is becoming increasingly difficult to sustain when the conditions for employment are either not met or only met on terms which are unacceptable. It also lies in the reconstruction of the meanings attached to retirement and old age. The notion, propounded by Beveridge, of retirement as a period of dependency has been replaced by an ideal (as yet fully experienced only by a minority) of retirement as a significant period of life, with a range of activity patterns open to individual choice (Kohli and Rein, 1991). Featherstone and Hepworth (1989) characterize this change as the 'modernization' of ageing, with the social reconstruction of middle age, this becoming more fluidly defined as 'mid-life' or the 'middle years'. Importantly, this period is increasingly defined and managed outside formal occupational roles: with the significance of caring responsibilities (for partners and elderly parents) for some; for others, the gradual emergence of new lifestyles built around changing patterns of consumption.

As suggested in Chapter 5, the notion of 'positive retirement' started to be questioned in the 1990s in the context of fears about the economic viability of ageing populations (World Bank, 1994). However, we would want to challenge both the basis for these fears and the way in which retirement has been marginalized as a potentially liberating phase within the life course. The case of sustaining this latter vision seems important to make: the institution of retirement was in many respects one of the 'triumphs' of the twentieth century. However, its development has always been open to questioning and retrenchment in periods of economic and ideological crisis. In the twenty-first century the task must surely be to reinsert the institution as occupying a central role within a modernized, and some would argue, postmodern life course.

Learning generations

An important source for reconstructing the basis for older age must also be located within the field of education and learning. A major contribution here has been made by specialists working in the field of educational gerontology, who have begun the important task of developing a framework for learning and education in the later years (Glendenning and Percy, 1990). The value of this work has to be placed in the context of the neglect of older adults within the educational system. The most authoritative estimates here – for Britain at least – have been produced by Schuller and Bostyn (1992) in their report for the Carnegie Inquiry into the Third Age. They estimated a figure of three-quarters of a million people in the 50–74 age group enrolled annually in some kind of formal adult education, with a similar number receiving some kind of organized training. Applying this level of participation to the total number of people aged 50 plus in the UK means that roughly 1 in 10 of the age group take part each year in formal learning. An equivalent number –

and probably rather more – engage in informal learning, that is activities which involve an intention to learn but which are not formally designated as such. The international evidence is summarized by Schuller and Bostyn as follows:

> No country appears outstanding in its educational provision specifically for older people, although the United States can claim to have pioneered interesting initiatives . . . and to have witnessed the strongest anti-discrimination statements. There are certain areas in which the UK can claim to be reasonably advanced, for example with the Open University and community education. Against this must be set the great overall deficit in the initial and continuing education and training of the population as a whole, now documented in numerous analyses. The contrast is sharpest with countries such as Scandinavia, where participation in adult education is so much more firmly part of the culture, with participation rates of 23 per cent and 16 per cent recorded for the 60–64 and 65–74 age groups in [the early 1980s]. (1992: 9)

The fact that nine out of 10 older people in Britain are disengaged from formal learning raises major issues about inequities in the distribution of educational resources. The figure is skewed to some extent by cohort factors, in particular (as Schuller and Bostyn highlight) the fact that two out of three of those aged 50 and over left school aged 15 and over. However, additional factors must include negative stereotypes about older people as potential learners; the impact of poverty and social class; and also the failure to develop education as a social right to be available throughout the life course. The last of these existing, despite the urging of UNESCO (in the 1970s) for lifelong learning, on the grounds that this would:

> . . . enable those who had left working life to retain their physical and intellectual faculties and to continue to participate in community life and also to give them access to fields which have not been open to them during their working life. (cited in Glendenning, 1990: 14)

In fact, the reality of the decades of the 1980s and 1990s was that, despite the expansion in the number of retirees, educational opportunities for older people were significantly reduced. The crisis in the university adult education sector had a disproportionate impact on older people, who comprise the largest group attending day and evening classes. Community education organized by local government has, historically, been a major provider of education for older people. Once again, this sector has faced contraction in its range of provision, despite the expansion in the numbers of potential participants. This contradiction has also been massively apparent in the 'Cinderella area' of pre-retirement education (PRE). Despite the publication of national surveys in the early 1980s urging improvement in terms of the quality and take-up of programmes (Coleman, 1982; Phillipson and Strang, 1983), there was almost certainly a decline during the 1980s in the numbers participating in PRE. Schuller and Bostyn (1992: 20) calculate a figure of 30,000 people participating annually in PRE, a derisory figure given the approximately 600,000 people in the cohort five years below state retirement age.

Taken overall, the figures highlighted above represent a massive exclusion of older people from learning opportunities which might add substantially to the quality of the 20 or more years spent in retirement. Given the chronic employment problems in the late 1970s and through the 1980s, governments were content to expand the number of retirees. At the same time, as we have seen, access to education programmes was reduced, and even the modest programmes to help people prepare for retirement were cut back.

Faced with this situation, it seems important to argue for a fresh perspective on the importance of older learners both to society and the economy. In respect of government responsibilities, some of the key policy issues have been summarized by Schuller and Bostyn as follows:

> [First] A clear policy statement on the rights of older people to a broad range of educational opportunity. [Second] All relevant educational bodies to have a clear obligation towards adult learners, including older adults. [Third] the duty on local education authorities to secure sufficient provision of adult education to be confirmed, accompanied by adequate resources. [Fourth] coordination of and support for distance learning providers, with particular reference to older learners with problems of mobility. (1992: 98–9)

These, and the many other policy proposals raised by these researchers, should be seen as a national priority. It would be an exaggeration to argue that without effective education provision the years in retirement are wasted. Older people have, in fact, been highly successful in promoting diverse and imaginative educational activities of their own. But there is a massive case for expanding the field, and drawing on the resources of older people in different ways throughout the community.

Interdependent generations

The argument for a different approach to issues such as financial support and learning opportunities in older age is closely bound up with a broader vision about how different generations view the last phase in the life course. Here, it is important to emphasize the extent to which a new approach is needed for describing the relationships between generations. The intemperate language of the 1980s and 1990s, which drew upon long-standing metaphors focusing on the burden of old age (Warnes,

1993), generated an oppressive vision of the future of population ageing. An alternative approach would, however, stress the interdependency of generations (Phillipson et al., 1986). This perspective would acknowledge ageing as a public concern to be shared equally across the life course. Above all, we should not 'off-load' the responsibilities for an ageing population to particular generations or cohorts – whether old, young or middle aged. Ageing is an issue *for* generations, but it is one to be solved *with* generations. Integrating older people across and within different social groups and institutions must rest upon this framework of generational cooperation and support.

Having stated this broad perspective, some major concerns do need to be acknowledged. For example, older people are – in late old age – highly vulnerable to abuse and neglect of different kinds. This issue has been of fairly long-standing attention in the USA, but has now emerged as an area of debate in the UK (Biggs et al., 1993; Bennett et al., 1997; Decalmer and Glendenning, 1997). Such abuse may occur in private households; it may also be present in communal settings of different kinds. The conditions for the development of abuse may have increased in the late twentieth century, first, with the growth in the numbers of people aged 85 and over; second, because of the growth in the numbers of small residential homes, these often being relatively isolated in urban as well as rural locations; third, because of pressures on family relationships, for example with the expectations placed upon informal carers by the development of policies in the field of community care.

The debate on abuse and neglect has in fact had positive as well as more negative connotations. The latter are perhaps obvious, with abuse against the old seemingly providing a reminder of the pervasive violence in personal relationships running through contemporary society. Regarding the former, mistreatment of the old has also led to questions about what precisely is the basis for a life free of abuse and neglect? How can people live a life without physical violence at one extreme, or verbal abuse at another? What is the basis for relationships which serve to empower and strengthen the rights of older people?

Another concern, one which may be bound up with the debate concerning abuse, revolves around the biological and physiological dependencies which affect people as they move through later life. In this regard, older people do experience profound changes to their bodies which raise many issues for the quality of daily living. However, the way in which society responds to these changes is of crucial importance. In our society people are given full accreditation as human beings only when they have reached a relatively high level of cognitive, biological and emotional development. This aspect of how human development is perceived has major implications for older people. Featherstone and Hepworth, for example, have suggested that:

If the process of becoming an acceptable human being is dependent upon these developments, the loss of cognitive and other skills produces the danger of social unacceptablity, unemployability and being labelled as less than fully human. Loss of bodily controls carries similar penalties of stigmatisation and ultimately exclusion. Deep [or late] old age is personally and socially disturbing because it holds out the prospect of the loss of some or all of these controls. Degrees of loss impair the capacity to be counted as a competent adult. Indeed, the failure of bodily controls also impairs other interactional skills, and the loss of real power through decline in these competencies may induce others to feel confident in treating the individual as a less than full adult. Carers may, for example, feel secure in the belief that the person 'inside' will not be able to return to wreak any vengeance on them whatever their former social status or class background. (1989: 261)

Hepworth and Featherstone are raising a wider point here about the extent to which the ageing process can be seen as a mask which conceals an enduring and more youthful self (see also Biggs, 1993). The tension here is between given functional capacities on the one hand, and personal identity on the other. In this context older people seem to be faced with a number of threats in a late modern age: first, identity, as argued throughout this book, is itself precarious – at any stage of life. People have constantly to recreate and reconstruct their identity – to maintain a narrative about themselves, as Giddens (1991) puts it. But in late old age the conditions for achieving this may be unavailable or denied to certain groups of people. Second, again as argued at different points in this study, the basis for identity in old age seems more unstable given the questioning of the narratives associated with the welfare state on the one hand, and retirement on the other. Third, maintaining identity is in any event a struggle for people who, by virtue of illness or their residential location, may be denied the support and interaction essential to reaffirming a sense of self and identity.

All these changes reinforce the case for focusing on the way in which generations – in a micro- as well as macro-sociological sense – need to establish close and supportive ties within themselves and between each other. Fostering this would seem to be an important goal for a number of groups, but especially for those charged with the delivery of different kinds of health and social services.

Following this, it is also clear that there is a major priority for rediscovering what Habermas (cited in Moody, 1992: 416) describes as: 'communicative ethics' based upon shared discourse among persons who respect each other's position in the process of communication. In this perspective, finding the 'correct answer' to an ethical dilemma may be less a matter of agreeing on abstract principles than it is a matter of sharing a commitment to free and open communication and work on behalf of institutional structures that support such communication.

Moody, however, notes that there are major obstacles to this which need to be overcome:

> This ideal standard of communication is admittedly very far from what we find in most arenas of contemporary life. Habermas has argued that it is characteristic of advanced industrialized societies that we encounter 'systematically distorted communications,' which serve to frustrate open communication . . . everywhere we find an evasion or falsification of discourse. Instead of open deliberation we see domination by power or manipulation. The development of human services for the ageing has followed precisely this pattern. For example, the rise of the nursing home industry does not empower older people to make decisions about their lives. Instead, the elderly become a new class of consumers subject to the expanding domination by professionals in [what Estes has termed] the 'Ageing Enterprise'. Instead of freedom, we have the 'colonization' of the life world in old age, and the last stage is emptied of any meaning beyond sheer biological survival. (1992: 417)

Moody here raises the issue that the new language of viewing older people as consumers has marginalized, rather than placed at the centre, questions relating to rights and empowerment. The older people we described in Chapter 4, who were moved from their long-stay ward to the community care home, were 'consumers' of health and social care, but they experienced this with catastrophic results. Growing old for them was a personal tragedy but it also involved (as C. Wright Mills (1970) would have said) public concerns as well. It is the broader dimension arising from their experience which has been the main theme of this book: people do need a secure anchorage for themselves. As already argued, this is important whether young and fit; frail and demented. At the end of the twentieth century, however, we are still trying to work out a suitable place for older people in the general scheme of things. For many older people that may not matter for some part of their old age. But for most there will come a point at which the limits to growing old are reached, not in the biological sense (which of course will always be there), but in the images and practices which society maintains about older people. Changing and transforming these limits will be a central issue for social policy in the twenty-first century.

10

CONCLUSION: EXCLUSION AND RESISTANCE IN THE SOCIOLOGY OF AGEING

The main concern of this study has been with developing a sociological account of changes to the context and experiences associated with growing old. A particular focus has been on developments over the past 50 years, these culminating in the crisis associated with the unravelling of the central institutions supporting old age. The legacy is certainly one of complexity and uncertainty about what is being carried forward into the twenty-first century: what sort of old age should be developed over the next, say, 50 years? What kind of relationships between generations do we want to encourage? What should be the balance between the state, at national and local levels, voluntary bodies, and individuals and their families, in respect of supporting the lives of older people?

The balance between these different elements was certainly disturbed in the 1980s and 1990s. The argument for the state limiting its responsibilities for old age was conveyed with some vigour by governments during this period. But the alternatives were neither so easily expressed nor satisfactory where they were developed. Attempts (by Conservative governments in Britain) at alternative funding – through the privatization of pensions – could be described as farcical, but this would belittle the anxiety created through the misselling of private schemes to thousands of individuals. The privatization of residential homes and community care – held out as a way of widening choice – failed to provide real security for late old age, with too many lives still blighted by worry and anxiety at a time when the effect of chronic illness is about as much as anyone (or any family) can be reasonably expected to bear.

The ending of the life course, this book has argued, remains still in great crisis, and a major task for the years ahead must be to restore vision and purpose to what is a genuine triumph of the preceding 100 years. For such a project to be successful, however, it is clear that significant hurdles must be overcome in how we conceptualize and respond to population ageing. Part of the excitement here is that this will require real collaboration from many disciplines, from biomedicine to the full range of the social sciences. This aspect of modernity, that which founded and developed gerontology, certainly maintains its relevance and should be encouraged. But it is also the argument of this book that a sociologically orientated, critical gerontology is also of great importance. Much work must be done, however, in respect of developing a sociology of old age, one that is sensitive and responsive to social structures on the one side, and to older people's own activities and lifestyles on the other.

Concerning the former, the argument, based on this study, is for developing a 'sociology of exclusion', one that focuses on the way in which identities in later life are controlled and managed within dominant social institutions. In the early twenty-first century, these are likely to focus around four types of exclusion: first, ideological, with the continuing alarmism and scapegoating associated with population ageing; second, economic, with the construction of regular crises, and threats to the funding of state pensions and other types of support; third, political, with the curtailment of civil rights in areas or zones (for example, retirement communities) where older people congregate; fourth, affective, with the failure to recognize the emotional needs associated with the various changes running through the life course.

These processes of exclusion raise significant issues for the sociology of old age and represent a major challenge as well to trends within mainstream gerontology. Their combined effect – examined in different ways throughout this book – has been to place severe restrictions on how old age has developed during the twentieth century. In the 1980s, the way in which growing old had been constructed was defined as a form of 'structured dependency'. The argument here was that the type of policy developments that had emerged in the post-war period – notably those associated with retirement and the organization of welfare – represented a form of 'institutional ageism'. The end result was the way in which the interests of the old became subordinate to those concerned with the management of industry and the economy.

The 'structured dependency' model was of great value in explaining many characteristics of ageing, especially at a time when the founding institutions of the welfare state retained their dominant role. However, the changes that began to take effect from the 1980s through to the 1990s have altered the terms of the debate. As argued in Chapter 4 of this book, the restructuring of those elements associated with 'organized capitalism' have had major consequences for a variety of social groups. Older people, it has been argued, have moved into a new of zone of indeterminacy, marginal to work and welfare. The implication of this is that in the twenty-first century – for a period at least – there will be rather different forms of exclusion operating than in the preceding 50 years. These will be of great importance for sociologists to study and learn about. Until now, social exclusion has tended to be examined from the standpoint of people placed at earlier points in the life course, with issues associated with disadvantages in the workplace, at school and in the home being the primary focus of concern. However, if the arguments developed in Chapter 4 are correct, then it is the exclusion of people at later points in the life course which may provide more telling insights regarding alterations to self and identity in a postmodern world.

Developing a sociology of exclusion is, then, one of the ways in which ageing might usefully be studied in the future. Equally, however, there is a case for focusing on what may be termed a 'sociology of daily living' as a way of understanding the nature of social ageing. Here it might be argued that the study of older age offers different kinds of opportunities for investigating social life, when compared with other age and social groups. On the one hand, it is certainly important to learn about the engagement of older people with dominant social institutions. Studies, for example, of the ways in which older people have formed political organizations in response to the experience of poverty and inadequate social and health care, now form an important part of gerontological research. Similarly, the way in which elderly people relate to different groups within the sphere of family and kinship relations has developed as an obvious tradition within social research.

There is, however, the prospect of another kind of study that can use the tools and methods of sociological studies. Older people now live predominantly in one-generation households – either with a partner or on their own. They may still relate strongly to primary groups such as the family, but for the organization of daily life their own self-activity is of great importance. Activities are more often than not done alone (reading, watching television, gardening) or with just one other person. Essentially, this is the world of micro-sociology, rather than the macro-sociology with which we are more familiar. But the sociology of this – the distinctive ways in which daily life is given shape and meaning – is still poorly understood. Older people are involved in sustaining their sense of self and identity in conditions that many yet to be defined as old would find difficult if not intolerable. In cultural terms, we find this hard to talk about or acknowledge. From the standpoint of writing this book, for example, it is certainly easier to discuss the statistics associated with the poverty of the old than it is to say something about the way in which daily life is constructed or managed. At one time this used to be talked about using words such as 'loneliness' and 'isolation'. But these were never adequate to convey the complexity of life in old age. Moreover, they ignored the sense in which describing the organization of daily life reveals as much about the way in which people 'resist' rather than succumb to the pressures associated with growing old. This type of research is, then, partly about developing a 'sociology of resistance':

focusing on the way in which older people challenge situations they are confronted with, but in what is often private rather than public settings.

These different points seem to the author to present a fresh and radical agenda for a sociology of ageing. Over the past 10 or 20 years, if the thesis of this book is correct, a new type of ageing has emerged, one that calls into question traditional social gerontological research. Overall, what is important to establish is that the way in which we construct ageing and older age is changing radically, and with it the identities, outlooks and potential of older people. The challenge for researchers is an exciting one: to document new lifestyles, institutions and identities among elderly people. Understanding the way in which growing old is being reconstructed, and its linkages to other areas of life and other institutions, is now a key task for social scientists to address. In this respect, studying the lives of older people has become a central concern for those involved in sociological as well as gerontological research and investigation.

BIBLIOGRAPHY

Abel-Smith, B. and Townsend, P. (1965) *The Poor and the Poorest*. London: Bell.

Abrams, P. (1982) *Historical Sociology*. Shepton Mallet: Open Books.

Achenbaum, W.A. (1978) *Old Age in the New Land: The American Experience Since 1790*. London: Johns Hopkins University Press.

Achenbaum, W.A. (1986) 'The meaning of risk, rights, and responsibility in aging America', in T. Cole and S. Gadow (eds), *What Does It Mean to Grow Old?* Durham, NC: Duke University Press. pp. 65–98.

Achenbaum, W.A. (1995) *Crossing Frontiers: Gerontology Emerges as a Science*. Cambridge: Cambridge University Press.

Adonis, A. (1998) 'If you think we've got problems', *Observer*. 18 January, p. 21.

Amann, A. (ed.) (1984) *Social-Gerontological Research in European Countries – History and Current Trends*. Berlin (West) and Vienna: German Centre of Gerontology. Berlin (West): Ludwig Boltzmann/Vienna: Institute of Social Gerontology and Life Span Research.

Arber, S. and Ginn, J. (1991) *Gender and Later Life*. London: Sage.

Arber, S. and Ginn, J. (1996) *Connecting Gender and Aging: A Sociological Approach*. Buckingham: Open University Press.

Arendell, T. and Estes, C.L. (1991) 'Older women in the post-Reagan era', in M. Minkler and C. Estes (eds), *Critical Perspectives on Aging*. New York: Baywood.

Armstrong, P., Glyn, A. and Harrison, J. (1984) *Capitalism Since World War II*. London: Fontana Paperbacks.

Atchley, R. (1971) 'Retirement and leisure participation', *The Gerontologist*, 11 (1): 13–17.

Atchley, R. (1976) *The Sociology of Retirement*. Cambridge, MA: Schenkman.

Atchley, R. (1982) 'Retirement: leaving the world of work', *Annals of the American Academy of Political and Social Sciences*, 464: 120–31.

Atchley, R. (1993) 'Critical perspectives on retirement', in T. Cole, W.A. Achenbaum, P. Jakobi, and R. Kastenbaum (eds), *Voices and Visions of Aging: Toward a Critical Gerontology*. New York: Springer.

Atchley, R. (1994) *Social Forces and Aging*. Belmont, CA: Wadsworth.

Atkinson, J. (1994) 'State pensions of today and tomorrow', *Welfare State Programme Discussion Paper 104*. London: Sticerd/London School of Economics.

Baars, J. (1991) 'The challenge of critical studies', *Journal of Aging Studies*, 5 (3): 219–43.

Bartley, M., Blane, D. and Charlton, J. (1997) 'Socioeconomic and demographic trends', in J. Charlton and M. Murphy (eds), *The Health of Adult Britain*

1841–1994. Decennial Supplement No. 12. London: Office of National Statistics. pp. 74–92.

Bauman, Z. (1992) *Intimations of Postmodernity*. London: Routledge & Kegan Paul.

Bauman, Z. (1996) *Postmodernity and its Discontents*. Oxford: Blackwell.

Beck, U. (1992) *Risk Society*. London: Sage.

Beck, U. (1994) 'The reinvention of politics', in U. Beck, A. Giddens and S. Lash (eds), *Reflexive Modernisation*. Cambridge: Polity.

Beck, U., Giddens, A. and Lash, S. (eds) (1994) *Reflexive Modernisation*. Cambridge: Polity.

Bengston, V. (1993) 'Is the "contract across generations" changing? Effects of population aging on obligations and expectations across age groups', in V. Bengston and V.W. Achenbaum (eds), *The Changing Contract Across Generations*. New York: Aldine de Gruyter. pp. 3–24.

Bengston, V. and Achenbaum, W.A. (eds) (1993) *The Changing Contract Across Generations*. New York: Aldine de Gruyter.

Bennett, G., Kingston, P. and Penhale, B. (1997) *The Dimensions of Elder Abuse*. London Macmillan.

Bernard, M. and Meade, K. (eds) (1993) *Women Come of Age*. London: Edward Arnold.

Bernard, M. and Phillips, J. (eds) (1997) *The Social Policy of Old Age*. London: Centre for Social Policy on Ageing.

Bertaux, D. (ed.) (1981) *Biography and Society: The Life History Approach in the Social Sciences*. Beverley Hills, CA: Sage.

Best, F. (1980) *Flexible Life Scheduling*. New York: Praeger.

Beveridge, W. (1942) *Social Insurance and Allied Services*. London: HMSO.

Beynon, H. (1975) *Working for Ford*. Wakefield: E.P. Publishing.

Biggs, S. (1993) *Understanding Ageing*. Buckingham: Open University Press.

Biggs, S. (1997) 'Choosing not to be old? Masks, bodies and identity management in later life', *Ageing and Society*, 17 (5): 553–70.

Biggs, S., Phillipson, C. and Kingston, P. (1993) *Old Age Abuse*. Buckingham: Open University Press.

Binstock, R. and Post, S. (eds) (1991) *Too Old For Health Care?* London: Johns Hopkins University Press.

Birren, J. (ed.) (1959) *The Handbook of Aging and the Individual: Psychological and Biological Aspects*. Chicago: University of Chicago Press.

Birren, J.E. (1996) 'History of gerontology', in J. Birren (ed.), *Encyclopaedia of Gerontology*, Vol. 1. San Diego: Academic Press.

Birren, J. and Clayton, V. (1975) 'History of gerontology', in D. Woodruff and J. Birren (eds), *Ageing: Scientific Perspectives and Social Issues*. New York: Van Nostrand. pp. 15–27.

Birren, J.E., Kenyon, G., Ruth, J.-E., Schroots, J.J.F. and Svensson, T. (eds) (1996) *Ageing and Biography: Explorations in Adult Development*. New York: Springer.

Blaikie, A. and MacNicol, J. (1989) 'Ageing and social policy: a twentieth century dilemma', in A.M. Warnes (ed.), *Human Ageing and Later Life*. London: Edward Arnold. pp. 69–82.

Blau, Z. (1973) *Old Age in a Changing Society*. New York: New Viewpoints.

Blumer, H. (1969) *Symbolic Interactionism*. Englewood Cliffs, NJ: Prentice-Hall.

Bone, M., Gregory, J., Gill, B. and Lader, D. (1992) *Retirement and Retirement Plans*. London: OPCS Social Survey Division.

Bornat, J., Phillipson, C. and Ward, S. (1985) *A Manifesto for Old Age*. London: Pluto Press.

Bradley, H. (1996) *Fractured Identities*. Cambridge: Polity.

Branson, N. and Heinemann, M. (1971) *Britain in the Nineteen Thirties*. London: Weidenfeld & Nicolson.

Brockelhurst, J.C. (ed.) (1978) *Textbook of Geriatric Medicine and Gerontology*. Edinburgh: Churchill Livingstone.

Brown, J. (1990) *Social Security for Retirement*. York: Joseph Rowntree Foundation.

Brown, R.A. (1957) 'Age and "paced" work', *Occupational Psychology*, 31 (1): 11–20.

Bulmer, M., Lewis, J. and Piachaud, D. (1989) *The Goals of Social Policy*. London: Unwin Hyman.

Burgess, E.W. (ed.) (1960) *Aging in Western Societies: A Survey of Social Gerontology*. Chicago: University of Chicago Press.

Burns, B. and Phillipson, C. (1986) *Drugs, Ageing and Society*. London: Croom Helm.

Bury, M. (1995) 'Ageing, gender and sociological theory', in S. Arber and J. Ginn (eds), *Connecting Gender and Ageing: A Sociological Approach*. Buckingham: Open University Press. pp. 15–29.

Bytheway, B. (1986) 'Making way: the disengagement of older workers', in C. Phillipson, P. Strang and M. Bernard (eds), *Dependency and Interdependency in Later Life*. London: Croom Helm.

Calasanti, T. (1996) 'Incorporating diversity: meanings, levels of research and implications for theory', *The Gerontologist*, 36 (2): 147–56.

Calasanti, T. and Zajicek, A. (1993) 'A socialist-feminist approach to ageing: embracing diversity', *Journal of Ageing Studies*, 7. 133–50.

Calhoun, R.B. (1978) *In Search of the New Old: Redefining Old Age in America 1945–70*. New York: Elsevier.

Callahan, D. (1987) *Setting Limits: Medical Goals in an Ageing Society*. New York: Touchstone Books.

Carboni, D. (1982) *Geriatric Medicine in the United States and Great Britain*. Westport, CT: Greenwood Press.

Carers National Association (1996) *Who Cares? Perceptions of Caring and Carers*. London: Carers National Association.

Cavan, R.S., Burgess, E.W. and Goldhamer, H. (1949) *Personal Adjustment in Old Age*. Chicago: Science Research Associates.

Chapman, S.J. and Hallsworth, M.M. (1909) *Unemployment: The Results of an Investigation Made in Lancashire and an Examination of the Reports of the Poor Law Commission*. Manchester: University of Manchester.

Chisholm, C. (1954) *Retire and Enjoy It*. London: Phoenix Books.

Clark, R. and Spengler, J. (1980) *The Economics of Individual and Population Ageing*. Cambridge: Cambridge University Press.

Clarke, P. (1996) *Britain 1900–1990*. London: Allen Lane.

Coates, K. and Silburn, K. (1970) *Poverty: The Forgotten Englishmen*. London: Penguin.

Cole, D. and Utting, J. (1962) *The Economic Circumstances of Old People*. London: Bell and Sons.

Cole, T. (1992) *The Journey of Life: A Cultural History of Aging in America*. Cambridge: Cambridge University Press.

Cole, T., Achenbaum, W.A., Jakobi, P. and Kastenbaum, R. (eds) (1993) *Voices and Visions of Aging: Toward a Critical Gerontology*. New York: Springer.

Cole, T., Van Tassell, D. and Kastenbaum, R. (eds) (1992) *Handbook of the Humanities and Aging*. New York: Springer.

Coleman, A. (1982) *Preparation for Retirement in England and Wales*. Leicester: National Institute of Adult Education in association with the Pre-Retirement Association of Great Britain and Northern Ireland. Ed. J. Groombridge.

Community Development Projects (1977) *The Costs of Industrial Change*. London: CDP.

Conrad, C. (1992) 'Old age in the modern and postmodern world', in T. Cole, D. Van Tassell and R. Kastenbaum (eds), *Handbook of the Humanities and Aging*. New York: Springer.

Corson, J. and McConnell, J. (1956) *Economic Needs of Older People*. New York: Twentieth Century Fund.

Cottam, R. (1954) 'Growing old', in *Living Longer: Some Social Aspects of the Problem of Old Age*. London: The National Council of Social Service.

Cowgill, D. and Holmes, L.D. (eds) (1972) *Aging and Modernization*. New York: Appleton-Century-Crofts.

Creedy, J. and Disney, R. (1989) 'The new pension scheme in Britain', in A. Dilnot and I. Walker (eds), *The Economics of Social Security*. Oxford: Oxford University Press. pp. 224–38.

Crook, S., Pakulski, J. and Waters, M. (1992) *Postmodernization: Change in Advanced Society*. London: Sage.

Cumming, E. and Henry, W.E. (1961) *Growing Old: The Process of Disengagement*. New York: Basic Books.

Dalley, G. (1993) 'Caring: a legitimate interest of older women', in M. Bernard and K. Meade (eds), *Women Come of Age*. London: Edward Arnold.

Daniel, W.W. (1982) *Whatever Happened to the Workers at Woolwich*. London: Political and Economic Planning.

Decalmer, P. and Glendenning, F. (eds) (1997) *The Mistreatment of Elderly People*. London: Sage.

Department of Health (1989) *Caring for People: Community Care in the next Decade and Beyond*, Cmnd. 849. London: HMSO.

Department of Health (1994) *NHS Hospital Activity Statistics: England 1983–94 – Statistical Bulletin*. London: Department of Health.

Department of Health and Social Security (1981) *Growing Older*, Cmnd. 8173. London: HMSO.

Department of Health and Office of Population Census and Surveys (1995) *The Government's Expenditure Plans 1995–96–1997–98: Departmental Report*, CM2812, London: HMSO.

Department of Social Security (1992) *Social Security Statistics 1992*. London: HMSO.

Department of Social Security (1993) *The Growth of Social Security*. London: HMSO.

Department of Social Security (1997) *Welfare Reform Focus File*. London: Central Office of Information.

Department of Social Security (1998) *A New Contract for Welfare*, Cm3805. London: Stationery Office.

Dex, S. and Phillipson, C. (1986) 'Social policy and the older worker', in C. Phillipson and A. Walker (eds), *Ageing and Social Policy: A Critical Assessment*. Aldershot: Gower Books.

Dilnot, A. (1997) 'Paying for government', ESRC Social Science Conference, 25 June, QEII Centre, London.

Disney, R., Grundy, E. and Johnson, P. (1997) *The Dynamics of Retirement*. Department of Social Security, Research Report No. 72. London: The Stationery Office.

Donahue, W., Orbach, H., Pollak, O. (1960) Retirement: the emerging social pattern, in C. Tibbitts (ed.), *The Handbook of Social Gerontology: Societal Aspects of Aging*. Chicago: University of Chicago Press.

Dowd, J.J. (1975) 'Aging as exchange: a preface to theory', *Journal of Gerontology*, 30 (5): 584–94.

Dychtwald, K. (1989) *Age Wave: The Challenges and Opportunities of an Aging America*. Los Angeles: Tarcher.

Easterlin, R.A. (1978) 'What will 1984 be like? Socio-economic implications of recent shifts in age structure', *Demography*, 15 (4): 397–432.

Elder, G. (1977) *The Alienated: Growing Old Today*. London: Writers and Readers Publishing Co-operative.

Emerson, A.R. (1959) ' The first year of retirement', *Occupational Psychology*, 33: 197–208.

Employment Department Group (1994) *Getting On: The Benefits of an Older Workforce*. London: EDG.

Ensor, R.C.K. (1950) 'The problem of quantity and quality in the British population', *Eugenics Review*, 42 (3): 128–35.

Ermisch, J. (1990) *Fewer Babies, Longer Lives*. York: Joseph Rowntree Foundation.

Estes, C. (1979) *The Aging Enterprise*. San Francisco: Jossey Bass.

Estes, C. (1986) 'The politics of aging in America', *Ageing and Society*, 6 (2): 121–34.

Estes, C. (1991) 'The new political economy of aging: introduction and critique', in M. Minkler and C. Estes (eds), *Critical Perspectives on Ageing: The Political and Moral Economy of Growing Old*. New York: Baywood.

Estes, C. (1993) 'The aging enterprise revisited', *The Gerontologist*, 33 (3): 292–8.

Estes, C. (1998) 'Critical gerontology and the new political economy of aging', in M. Minkler and C. Estes (eds), *Critical Gerontology: Perspectives from Political and Moral Economy*. New York: Baywood.

Estes, C. and Binney, E. (1989) 'The biomedicalization of aging: dangers and dilemmas', *The Gerontologist*, 29 (5): 587–98.

Estes, C., Gerard L., Zones, J.S. and Swan, J.S. (1984) *Political Economy, Health and Ageing*. Boston: Little, Brown.

Estes, C. and Linkins, K.W. (1997) 'Devolution and aging policy: racing to the bottom in long-term care', *International Journal of Health Services*, 27 (3): 427–42.

Estes, C., Linkins, K. and Binney, E. (1996) 'The political economy of aging', in R. Binstock and L. George (eds), *Handbook of Ageing and the Sciences*. New York: Academic Press. pp. 346–61.

Estes, C.L., Swan, J.H. and Associates (1993) *The Long Term Care Crisis*. Newbury Park, CA: Sage.

Falkingham, J. and Victor, C. (1991) 'The myth of the Woopie? Incomes, the elderly and targeting the elderly', *Ageing and Society*, 11 (4): 471–93.

Featherstone, M. (1987) 'Leisure, symbolic power and the life course' in D. Jary, S. Home and A. Tomlinson (eds), *Sport, Leisure and Social Relations*. London: Routledge.

Featherstone, M. and Hepworth, M. (1989) 'Ageing and old age: reflections on the postmodern life course', in B. Bytheway, T. Keil, P. Allat and A. Bryman (eds), *Becoming and Being Old*. London: Sage.

Featherstone, M. and Wernick, A. (1995) *Images of Ageing*. London: Routledge.

Fiegehen, G. (1986) 'Income after retirement', *Social Trends no. 16*. Central Statistical Office. London: HMSO.

Fennell, G., Phillipson, C. and Evers, H. (1988) *The Sociology of Old Age*. Buckingham: Open University Press.

Finch, J. (1989) *Family Obligations and Social Change*. Cambridge: Polity Press.

Fischer, D.H. (1977) *Growing Old in America*. New York: Oxford University Press.

Fogarty, M. (ed.) (1975) *40 to 60: How We Waste the Middle Aged*. London: Centre for Studies in Social Policy/Bedford Square Press.

Freter, H.J., Kohli, M. and Wolf, J. (1987) *Early Retirement and Work after Retirement*. Berlin: Freie Universität Berlin.

Friedmann, E. and Adamchak, D. (1983) 'Societal aging and intergenerational support systems', in A-M. Guillemard (ed.), *Old Age and the Welfare State*. New York: Sage.

Giddens, A. (1991) *Modernity and Self-Identity*. Oxford: Polity Press.

Ginn, J. and Arber, S. (1995) 'Moving the goalposts: the impact on British women of raising their state pension to 65', *Social Policy Review*, No. 7. London: Social Policy Association.

Glendenning, F. (1990) 'The emergence of educational gerontology', in F. Glendenning and K. Percy (eds), *Ageing Education and Society*. Keele: Association for Educational Gerontology. pp. 13–23.

Glendenning, F. and Percy, K. (eds) (1990) *Ageing, Education and Society*. Keele: Association for Educational Gerontology.

Glendinning, C. (1992) 'Employment and "community care": policies for the 1990s', *Work, Employment and Society*, 6 (1): 103–12.

Glennerster, H. and Hills, J. (eds) (1998) *The State of Welfare: The Economics of Social Spending*. Oxford: Oxford University Press.

Goodin, R. and Dryzek, J. (1987) 'Risk-taking and social justice: the motivational foundations of the post-war welfare state', in R. Goodin and J. Le Grand (eds), *Not Only the Poor: The Middle Classes and the Welfare State*. London: Allen & Unwin.

Gordon, C. (1988) *The Myth of Family Care? The Elderly in the 1930s*. STICERD, Welfare State Programme WSP/29. London: London School of Economics.

Gouldner, A. (1971) *The Coming Crisis of Western Sociology*. London: Heinemann.

Government Actuary (1990) *National Insurance Fund Long Term Financial Estimates*. London: HMSO.

Graebner, W. (1980) *A History of Retirement*. New Haven, CT: Yale University Press.

Grant, L. (1998) *Remind Me Who I Am Again*. London: Granta Books.

Green, B. (1993) *Gerontology and the Construction of Old Age*. New York: Aldine De Gruyter.

Griew, S. (1964) *Job Re-Design*. Paris: OECD.

Grimley-Evans, J. (1997) 'Geriatric medicine: a brief history', *British Medical Journal*, 315 (7115): 1075–7.

Gubrium, J.F. (1986) *Oldtimers and Alzheimer's: The Descriptive Organization of Senility*. Greenwich, CT: Jai Press.

Gubrium, J.F. (1993) 'Voice and context in a new gerontology', in T. Cole, W.A. Achenbaum, P. Jakobi and R. Kastenbaum (eds), *Voices and Visions of Aging: Toward a Critical Gerontology*. New York: Springer.

Gubrium, J. and Wallace, J.B. (1990) 'Who theorises age', *Ageing and Society*, 10 (2): 131–50.

Guillemard, A-M. (ed.) (1983) *Old Age and the Welfare State*. New York: Sage.

Guillemard, A-M. (1989) 'The trend towards early labour force withdrawal and the reorganisation of the life course', in P. Johnson, C. Conrad and D. Thomson (eds), *Workers versus Pensioners: Intergenerational Justice in an Ageing World*. Manchester: Manchester University Press.

Haber, C. and Gratton, B. (1993) *Old Age and the Search for Security*. Bloomington, IN: Indiana University Press.

Habermas, J. (1971) *Knowledge and Human Interests*. London: Heinemann.

Hancock, R., Jarvis, C. and Mueller, G. (1995) *The Outlook for Incomes in Retirement*. London: Age Concern Institute of Gerontology.

Hancock, R. and Weir, P. (1994) *More Ways than Means: A Guide to Pensioners' Incomes in Great Britain during the 1980s*. London: Age Concern Institute of Gerontology

Hannah, L. (1986) *Inventing Retirement*. Cambridge: Cambridge University Press.

Harper, S. and Thane, P. (1989) 'The consolidation of old age as a phase in life, 1945–1965', in M. Jefferys (ed.), *Growing Old in the Twentieth Century*. London: Routledge.

Harrington, M. (1963) *The Other America*. Baltimore: Penguin.

Havighurst, R.J. (1954) 'Flexibility and the social roles of the retired', *American Journal of Sociology*, 59 (1, 2): 309–11.

Health Education Authority (1994) *Investing in Older Workers*. London: HEA.

Hennessy, P. (1993) *Never Again: Britain 1945–1951*. London: Vintage Books.

Henretta, J. (1994) 'Recent trends in retirement', *Reviews in Clinical Gerontology*, 4 (1): 71–81.

Heron, A. (1962) 'Preparation for retirement: a new phase in occupational development', *Occupational Psychology*, 35 (1, 2): 1–9.

Heron, A. and Chown, S.M. (1960) 'Semi-skilled and over forty', *Occupational Psychology*, 33 (4): 263–74.

Hewitt, P. (1993) *About Time: The Revolution in Work and Family Life*. London: Rivers Oram Press.

Hill, M. (1993) *The Welfare State in Britain*. Aldershot: Edward Elgar.

Hills, J. (1993) *The Future of Welfare: A Guide to the Debate*. York: Joseph Rowntree Foundation.

Hills, J. (1995) 'Funding the welfare state', *Oxford Review of Economic Policy*, 11 (3): 27–43.

Hills, J. (1996) 'Does Britain have a welfare generation', in A. Walker (ed.), *The New Generational Contract: Intergenerational Relations, Old Age and Welfare*. London: UCL Press.

Hills, J. (1997) *The Future of Welfare: A Guide to the Debate*. Revised edn. York: Joseph Rowntree Foundation.

Hobsbawm, E. (1994) *Age of Extremes*. London: Michael Joseph.

Hobsbawm, E. (1997) 'To see the future, look at the past', *Guardian*, 7 June, p. 21.

Hochschild, A.R. (1975) 'Disengagement theory: a critique and proposal', *American Sociological Review*, 40 (October): 533–69.

Homer, P. and Holstein, M. (eds) (1990) *A Good Old Age?* New York: Touchstone Books.

Hooyman, N. and Kiyak, H. (1991) *Social Gerontology: A Multi-Disciplinary Perspective*. London: Allyn & Bacon.

House of Commons (1995) *Long Term Care: NHS Responsibilities for Meeting Continuing Health Care Needs*. First Report. Session 1995–1996, HC 19-1, Annex 2. London: HMSO.

House of Commons Health Committee (1994) *Memorandum from the Department of Health on Public Expenditure on Health and Personal Social Services*. First Special Report, Session 1993–4, HC617. London: HMSO.

Hutton, W. (1996) *The State We're In*. London: Vintage Books.

Institute of Personnel Management (1993) *Statement on Age and Employment*. London: IPM.

International Association of Gerontology (1954) *Old Age in the Modern World: Report of the Third Congress*. London: E. & S. Livingstone.

International Labour Organisation (1989) *From Pyramid to Pillar – Population Change and Social Security in Europe*. London: ILO.

Itzin, C. and Phillipson, C. (1993) *Age Barriers at Work*. Solihull: METRA.

Jackson, B. (1968) *Working Class Community*. London: Routledge & Kegan Paul.

Jamieson, A., Harper, S. and Victor, C. (1997) *Critical Approaches to Ageing and Later Life*. Buckingham: Open University Press.

Johnson, M. (1976) 'That was your life: a biographical approach to later life', in J.M.A. Munnichs, W.J.A. Van Den Heuval (eds), *Dependency and Interdependency in Old Age*. Hague: Martinus Nijhoff.

Johnson, P. (1989) 'The structured dependency of the elderly: a research note', in M. Jeffries (ed.), *Growing Old in the Twentieth Century*. London: Routledge.

Johnson, P., Conrad, C. and Thomson, D. (eds) (1989) *Workers versus Pensioners: Intergenerational Justice in an Ageing World*. Manchester: Manchester University Press in association with the Centre for Economic and Policy Research.

Johnson, P. and Falkingham, J. (1992) *Ageing and Economic Welfare*. London: Sage.

Kaminsky, M. (1993) 'Definitional ceremonies: depolitizing and reenchanting the culture of age', in T. Cole, W.A. Achenbaum, P. Jakobi and R. Kastenbaum (eds), *Voices and Visions of Aging: Toward a Critical Gerontology*. New York: Springer.

Katz, S. (1996) *Disciplining Old Age*. Charlottesville, VA: University Press of Virginia.

Kaufman, S.R. (1986) *The Ageless Self: Sources of Meaning in Later Life*. Madison, WI: University of Wisconsin Press.

Kenyon, G. (1996) 'Ethical issues in ageing and biography', *Ageing and Society*, 16 (6): 659–76.

Kincaid, J. (1973) *Poverty and Equality in Britain: A Study of Social Security and Taxation*. London: Pelican.

Kleemeier, R.W. (ed.) (1961) *Ageing and Leisure: A Research Perspective into the Meaningful Use of Time*. New York: Oxford University Press.

Kohli, M. (1986) 'The world we forgot: an historical review of the life course', in V.W. Marshall (ed.), *Later Life: The Social Psychology of Aging*. London: Sage.

Kohli, M. (1988) 'Ageing as a challenge to sociological theory', *Ageing and Society*, 8 (4): 367–95.

Kohli, M. and Rein, M. (1991) 'The changing balance of work and retirement', in M. Kohli, M. Rein. A.-M. Guillemard and H. Van Gunsteren (eds), *Time for Retirement: Comparative Studies of Early Exit from the Labour Force*. Cambridge: Cambridge University Press.

Kohli, M., Rein, M., Guillemard, A.-M. and Gunsteren, H. (1991) *Time for Retirement: Comparative Studies of Early Exit from the Labour Force*. Cambridge: Cambridge University Press.

Kuhn, M. (1991) *No Stone Unturned: The Life and Times of Maggie Kuhn*. New York: Ballantine.

Kumar, K. (1995) *From Post-Industrial to Post-Modern Society*. Oxford: Basil Blackwell.

Kumashiro, M. (1995) *The Paths to Productive Ageing*. London: Taylor & Francis.

Laczko, F. (1987) 'Older workers, unemployment and the discouraged worker effect', in S. Di Gregorio (ed.), *Social Gerontology: New Directions*. London: Croom Helm.

Laczko, F. (1990) 'New poverty and the old poor: pensioners' incomes in the European Community', *Ageing and Society*, 10 (3): 261–77.

Laczko, F. and Phillipson, C. (1991) *Changing Work and Retirement*. Milton Keynes: Open University Press.

Lash, S. (1994) 'Reflexivity and its doubles: structure, aesthetics, community', in U. Beck, A. Giddens and S. Lash (eds), *Reflexive Modernisation*. Cambridge: Polity.

Lash, S. and Urry, J. (1987) *The End of Organised Capitalism*. Cambridge: Polity.

Laslett, P. (1983) *The World We Have Lost – Further Explored*. Third edn. London: Methuen.

Laslett, P. (1989) *A Fresh Map of Life*. London: Weidenfeld and Nicolson.

Lee, G. (1985) 'Kinship and social support: the case of the United States', *Aging and Society*, 5 (4): 19–38.

Le Gros Clark, F. (1966) *Work, Age and Leisure: Causes and Consequences of the Shortened Working Life*. London: Michael Joseph.

Leonard, P. (1984) *Personality and Ideology*. London: Macmillan.

Leonard, P. (1997) *Postmodern Welfare*. London: Sage.

Lipton, H. and Lee, P. (1988) *Drugs and the Elderly*. Stanford: Stanford University Press.

Longman, P. (1987) *Born to Pay*. Boston, MA: Houghton Mifflin.

Longmate, N. (1974) *The Workhouse*. London: Temple Smith.

Lowe, R. (1993) *The Welfare State in Britain since 1945*. London: Macmillan.

Lynott, R. and Lynott, P.P. (1996) 'Tracing the course of theoretical development in the sociology of aging', *The Gerontologist*, 36 (6): 749–60.

Mackay, D.I. (1972) 'Redundancy and re-engagement: a study of car workers', *Manchester School of Economic and Social Studies*, XL (3): 295–312.

Maddox, G. (1966) 'Retirement as a social event', in J.C. McKinney and F.T. de Vyer (eds), *Aging and Social Policy*. New York: Appleton Century-Crofts.

Mannheim, K. (1952) 'The problem of generations', *The Essays on the Sociology of Knowledge*. London: Routledge & Kegan Paul.

Marmor, T., Mashaw, J. and Harvey, P. (1990) *America's Misunderstood Welfare State*. New York: Basic Books.

Marshall, T.H. (1949) 'Citizenship and social class', republished in *Sociology at the Crossroads*. London: Heinemann.

McGoldrick, A. and Cooper, C. (1989) *Early Retirement*. Aldershot: Gower.

McGregor, A. and Sproull, A. (1992) 'Employers and the flexible workforce', *Employment Gazette*, May: 225–34.

McLeod, J. (1997) *Narrative and Psychotherapy*. London: Sage.

Means, R. (1986) 'The development of social services for elderly: historical perspectives', in C. Phillipson and A. Walker (eds), *Ageing and Social Policy: A Critical Assessment*. Aldershot: Gower. pp. 87–108.

Means, R. and Smith, R. (1995) *The Development of Welfare Services for Elderly People*. London: Croom Helm.

Midland Bank (1985) 'Prospects for the pharmaceutical industry', *Midland Bank Review*, Summer, 7–16.

Mills, C. Wright (1970) *The Sociological Imagination*. London: Penguin.

Minichiello, V., Chappell, N., Kendig, H. and Walker, A. (eds) (1996) *Sociology of Ageing: International Perspectives*. Melbourne: International Sociological Association, Research Committee on Ageing.

Ministry of Labour and National Service (1959) *Annual Report for 1958*, Cmnd. 745. London: HMSO.

Minkler, M. (1991) 'Generational equity and the new victim blaming', in M. Minkler and C. Estes (eds), *Critical Perspectives on Aging*. New York: Baywood.

Minkler, M. (1996) 'Critical perspectives on ageing: new challenges for gerontology', *Ageing and Society*, 16 (4): 467–87.

Minkler, M. and Cole, T. (1998) 'Political and moral economy: getting to know one another', in M. Minkler and C. Estes (eds), *Critical Gerontology: Perspectives from Political and Moral Economy*. New York: Baywood.

Minkler, M. and Estes, C. (eds) (1991) *Critical Perspectives on Ageing: The Political and Moral Economy of Growing Old*. New York: Baywood.

Minkler, M. and Estes, C. (eds) (1998) *Critical Gerontology: Perspectives from Political and Moral Economy*. New York: Baywood.

Minkler, M. and Robertson, A. (1991) 'The ideology of age/race wars: deconstructing a social problem', *Ageing and Society*, 11 (1): 1–22.

Moody, H.R. (1988) 'Toward a critical gerontology: the contribution of the humanities to theories of ageing', in J.E. Birren and V.L. Bengston (eds), *Emergent Theories of Aging*. New York: Springer. pp. 19–40.

Moody, H.R. (1992) 'Gerontology and critical theory', *The Gerontologist*, 32 (3): 294–5.

Moody, H.R. (1993) 'Overview: what is critical gerontology and why is it important?', in T. Cole, W.A. Achenbaum, P. Jakobi and R. Kastenbaum (eds), *Voices and Visions of Ageing: Toward a Critical Gerontology.* New York: Springer.

Moody, H.R. (1998) *Aging: Concepts and Controversies.* Thousand Oaks, CA: Pine Forge Press.

Morgan, K.O. (1984) *Labour in Power.* Oxford: Oxford University Press.

Morgan, L. and Kunkel, S. (1998) *Aging: The Social Context.* Thousand Oaks, CA: Pine Forge Press.

Murrell, K.F.H. (1959) 'Major problems of industrial gerontology', *Journal of Gerontology,* 14: 216.

Myles, J. (1984) *Old Age in the Welfare State: The Political Economy of Public Pensions.* Lawrence, KS: University Press of Kansas.

Myles, J. (1996) 'Social security and support of the elderly: the Western experience', in J. Quadagno and D. Street (eds), *Ageing for the Twenty-First Century.* New York: St Martin's Press. pp. 381–97.

National Pensioners Convention (1998) *Pensions Not Poor Relief.* London: NPC.

Naylor, P. (1990) *Age No Barrier.* Solihull: Metropolitan Authorities Recruitment Agency.

Neugarten, B.L. and Hagestad, G.O. (1976) 'Age and the life course', in R. Binstock and E. Shanas (eds), *Handbook of Aging and the Social Sciences.* New York: Van Nostrand Reinhold. pp. 35–55.

Neugarten, B. and Neugarten, D. (1986) 'Changing meanings of age in the ageing society', in A. Pifer and L. Bronte (eds), *Our Ageing Society: Paradox and Promise.* New York: Norton. pp. 33–52.

Nichols, T. and Beynon, H. (1977) *Living with Capitalism.* London: Routledge & Kegan Paul.

Nisbet, R. (1969) *Social Change and History.* New York: Oxford University Press.

Novack, T. (1988) *Poverty and the State.* Buckingham: Open University Press.

OECD (1988) *Ageing Populations: The Social Policy Implications.* Paris: OECD.

OECD (1998) *The Employment Outlook.* Paris: OECD.

Offe, C. (1994) *Contradictions of the Welfare State.* London: Hutchinson.

Offe, C. and Heinze, R. (1991) *Beyond Employment.* Oxford: Policy Press.

Office of Fair Trading (1997) *Inquiry into Pensions.* London: OFT.

Office of National Statistics (1997) 'British labour force projections: 1997–2006', *Labour Market Trends,* 105 (2): 51–68.

O'Reilly, J. and Caro, F. (1994) 'Productive ageing: an overview of the literature', *Journal of Ageing and Social Policy,* 6 (3): 39–71.

Ovrebo, B. and Minkler, M. (1993) 'The lives of older women: perspectives from political economy and the humanities', in T. Cole, W.A. Achenbaum, P. Jakobi and R. Kastenbaum (eds), *Voices and Visions of Ageing: Toward a Critical Gerontology.* New York: Springer. pp. 289–309.

Owen, A.D.K. (1935) 'Employees' retirement pension schemes in Great Britain', *International Labour Review,* 32 (1): 80–99.

Palmer, J. and Gould, S. (1986) 'Economic consequences of population ageing', in A. Pifer and L. Bronte (eds), *Our Ageing Society: Paradox and Promise.* New York: Norton. pp. 367–90.

Palmore, E., Burchett, B., Fillenbaum, G., George, L. and Wallman, L. (1985) *Retirement: Causes and Consequences.* New York: Springer.

Pampel, F. (1998) *Aging, Social Inequality and Public Policy.* Thousand Oaks, CA: Pine Forge Press.

Parker, G. and Clarke, H. (1997) *Attitudes and Behaviours Towards Financial Planning for Care in Old Age.* Leicester: Nuffield Community Studies Unit, University of Leicester.

Parker, R. (1990) 'Elderly people and community care: the policy background', in I. Sinclair, R. Parker, D. Leat and J. Williams (eds), *The Kaleidoscope of Care.* London: HMSO. pp. 5–22.

Passuth, P. and Bengston, V. (1996) 'Sociological theories of aging: current perspectives and future directions', in J. Quadagno and D. Street (eds), *Ageing for the Twenty-First Century.* New York: St Martin's Press.

Pension Provision Group (1998) *We all Need Pensions – the Prospects for Future Provision: A Summary.* London: Department of Social Security.

Phillips, J. (ed.) (1995) *Working Carers and Older People.* Aldershot: Avebury.

Phillips Report (1954) *Report of the Committee on the Economic and Financial Problems of the Provision for Old Age,* Cmnd. 933. London: HMSO.

Phillipson, C. (1978) 'The experience of retirement: a sociological analysis'. PhD thesis, University of Durham.

Phillipson, C. (1981) 'Pre-retirement education: the British and American experience', *Ageing and Society,* 1 (3): 392–414.

Phillipson, C. (1982) *Capitalism and the Construction of Old Age.* London: Macmillan.

Phillipson, C. (1990) 'Intergenerational relations: conflict or consensus in the twenty-first century', *Policy and Politics,* 19 (1): 27–36.

Phillipson, C. (1991) 'The social construction of old age: perspectives from political economy', *Reviews in Clinical Gerontology,* 1 (4): 403–10.

Phillipson, C. (1993) 'The sociology of retirement', in J. Bond, P. Coleman and S. Peace (eds), *Ageing and Society: An Introduction to Social Gerontology.* London: Sage.

Phillipson, C. (1994) 'The modernisation of the life course: implications for social security and older people', in S. Baldwin and J. Falkingham, *Social Security and Social Change: New Challenges to the Beveridge Model.* Hemel Hempstead: Harvester Wheatsheaf.

Phillipson, C. (1996) 'Interpretations of ageing: perspectives from humanistic gerontology', *Ageing and Society,* 16 (3): 359–69.

Phillipson, C. (1998) 'The social construction of retirement: perspectives from critical theory and political economy', in M. Minkler and C. Estes, *Critical Gerontology: Perspectives from Political and Moral Economy.* New York: Baywood.

Phillipson, C., Bernard, M., Phillips, J. and Ogg, J. (forthcoming) 'The family and community life of older people: household structure and social networks in three urban areas', *Ageing and Society,* 18.

Phillipson, C., Bernard, M. and Strang, P. (eds) (1986) *Dependency and Interdependency in Old Age: Theoretical Perspectives and Policy Alternatives.* London: Croom Helm.

Phillipson, C. and Strang, P. (1983) *The Impact of Pre-Retirement Education.* Keele: Department of Adult Education, University of Keele.

Phillipson, C. and Walker, A. (eds) (1986) *Ageing and Social Policy: A Critical Assessment.* Aldershot: Gower.

Phillipson, C. and Walker, A. (1987) 'The case for critical gerontology', in S. DeGregorio (ed.), *Social Gerontology: New Directions*. London: Croom Helm.

Pierson, C. (1991) *Beyond the Welfare State*. Cambridge: Polity.

Porter, R. (1984) 'Do we really need doctors', *New Society*, 69: 87–9.

Pratt, H.J. (1993) *Gray Agendas*. Ann Arbor, MI: University of Michigan Press.

Preston, S. (1984) 'Children and the elderly: divergent paths for America's dependants', *Demography*, 21 (November): 435–58.

Quadagno, J. (1986) 'The transformation of old-age security', in D. Van Tassell and P. Stearns (eds), *Old Age in Bureaucratic Society*. Westport, CT: Greenwood Press. pp. 129–55.

Quadagno, J. (1996) 'Generational equity and the politics of the welfare state', in J. Quadagno and D. Street (eds), *Aging for the Twenty-First Century*. New York: St Martin's Press. pp. 398–418.

Quadagno, J. and Hardy, M. (1995) 'Work and retirement', in R. Binstock and L. George (eds), *Handbook of Aging and the Social Sciences*. Fourth edn. New York: Academic Press.

Quadagno, J. and Street, D. (eds) (1996) *Aging for the Twenty-First Century*. New York: St Martin's Press.

Ray, R. (1996) 'A postmodern perspective on feminist gerontology', *The Gerontologist*, 36 (5): 674–80.

Rein, M. (1991) 'Retirement and the moral economy: an historical interpretation of the German case', in M. Minkler and C. Estes (eds), *Critical Perpsectives on Aging: The Political and Moral Economy of Growing Old*. New York: Baywood.

Richardson, I.M. (1956) 'Retirement: a socio-medical study of 244 men', *Scottish Medical Journal*, 1: 381–91.

Riley, M., Johnson, M. and Foner, A. (1972) *Aging and Society Vol. 3: A Sociology of Age Stratification*. New York: Russell State Foundation.

Ritchie, J. and Barrowclough, R. (1983) *Paying for Equalisation*. Manchester: Equal Opportunities Commission/Social and Community Planning Research.

Roberts, N. (1970) *Our Future Selves*. London: Allen & Unwin.

Robertson, A. (1991) 'The politics of Alzheimer's disease: a case study in apocalyptic demography', in M. Minkler and C. Estes (eds), *Critical Perspectives on Aging: The Political and Moral Economy of Growing Old*. New York: Baywood. pp. 135–50.

Robertson, A. (1998) 'Beyond apocalyptic demography: toward a moral economy of interdependence', in M. Minkler and C. Estes, *Critical Gerontology: Perspectives from Political and Moral Economy*. New York: Baywood. pp. 55–74.

Rowntree, S. (1947) *Old People: Report of a Survey Committee on the Problems of Ageing and the Care of Old People*. London: Nuffield Foundation.

Rowntree, S.B. and Lasker, B. (1911) *Unemployment: A Social Study*. London: Macmillan.

Royal Commission on Population (1949) *Report*. London: HMSO.

Ruth, J.-E. and Kenyon, G. (1996a) 'Introduction to special issue on ageing, biography and practice', *Ageing and Society*, 16 (6): 653–8.

Ruth, J.-E. and Kenyon, G. (1996b) 'Biography in adult development and aging', in J.E. Birren, G.M. Kenyon, J.-E. Ruth, J.J.F. Schroots and T. Svensson (eds), *Aging and Biography: Explorations in Adult Development*. New York: Springer. pp. 1–20.

Salvage, A.V., Vetter, R.J. and Jones, D.A. (1989) 'Opinions concerning residential care', *Age and Ageing*, 18: 380–6.

Schaie, K.W. and Achenbaum, W.A. (eds) (1993) *Societal Impact on Aging*. New York: Springer.

Schuller, T. (1989) 'Work-ending: employment and ambiguity in later life', in B. Bytheway, T. Keil, P. Allat and A. Bryman (eds), *Becoming and Being Old*. London: Sage.

Schuller, T. and Bostyn, A.-M. (1992) 'Learning, education and training in the third age'. Research paper no. 3, Carnegie Inquiry into the Third Age, Dunfermline.

Schultz, J. (1980) *The Economics of Aging*. Belmont, CA: Wadsworth.

Schultz, J. (1991) 'Epilogue: the "buffer years": market incentives and evolving retirement policies', in J. Myles and J. Quadagno (eds), *States, Labour Markets, and the Future of Old Age Policy*. Philadelphia, PA: Temple University Press.

Schultz, J., Borowski, A. and Crown, C. (1991) *The Economics of Population Ageing*. New York: Auburn House.

Sennett, R. and Cobb, J. (1972) *The Hidden Injuries of Class*. Cambridge: Cambridge University Press.

Shanas, E. (1979) 'The family as a social support system in old age', *The Gerontologist*, 19 (1): 169–74.

Shaw, J. (1971) *On Our Conscience: The Plight of the Elderly*. London: Penguin.

Sheldon, J.H. (1948) *The Social Medicine of Old Age*. London: Nuffield Foundation.

Siegel, S.R. and Rives, J.M. (1978) 'Characteristics of existing and planned pre-retirement programs', *Aging and Work*, 1 (2): 93–9.

Slater, G. (1930) *Poverty and the State*. London: Constable.

Social Trends (1998) London: HMSO.

Stearns, P. (1975) *Lives of Labour: Work in a Maturing Industrial Society*. London: Croom Helm.

Stearns, P. (1977) *Old Age in European Society: The Case of France*. London: Croom Helm.

Stevenson, J. (1977) *Social Conditions in Britain between the Wars*. London: Penguin.

Stone, L. and Minkler, M. (1984) 'The socio-political context of women's retirement', in M. Minkler and C. Estes (eds), *Political Economy of Aging*. New York: Baywood.

Taylor, C. (1989) *Sources of the Self*. Cambridge: Cambridge University Press.

Taylor, P. and Walker, A. (1993) *Age and Employment: Policies, Attitudes and Practice*. London: Institute of Personnel Management.

Taylor, P. and Walker, A. (1995) 'Utilising older workers', *Employment Gazette*, April: 141–5.

Thane, P. (1978) 'Non-contribution versus insurance pensions 1878–1908', in P. Thane (ed.), *The Origins of British Social Policy*. London: Croom Helm. pp. 84–106.

Thomas, W. and Znaniecki, F. (1966 [1918–1920]) *The Polish Peasant in Europe and America*. 5 Vols. Boston, MA: Gorham Press.

Thompson, F. (1973 [1945]) *Lark Rise to Candleford*. London: Penguin.

Thompson, P. (1975) *The Edwardians*. London: Weidenfeld & Nicolson.

Thompson, P., Itzin, C. and Abendstern, M. (1990) *I Don't Feel Old*. Oxford: Oxford University Press.

Thomson, D. (1989) 'The welfare state and generational conflict: winners and losers', in P. Johnson, C. Conrad and D. Thomson (eds), *Workers versus Pensioners: Intergenerational Justice in an Ageing World*. Manchester: Manchester University Press in association with the Centre for Economic and Policy Research. pp. 33–56.

Thomson, D. (1996) *Selfish Generations? How Welfare States Grow Old*. Cambridge: White Horse Press.

Tibbitts, C. (ed.) (1960) *The Handbook of Social Gerontology: Societal Aspects of Aging*. Chicago: University of Chicago Press.

Timmins, N. (1996) *The Five Giants: A Biography of the Welfare State*. London: Fontana.

Titmuss, R.M. (1955) 'Pension systems and population change', *Political Quarterly*, 26: 152–66.

Titmuss, R. (1963) *Essays on the Welfare State*. Second edn. London: Allen & Unwin.

Touraine, A. (1995) *Critique of Modernity*. Oxford: Blackwell.

Townsend, P. (1955) 'The anxieties of retirement', *Transactions of the Association of Industrial Medical Officers*, April.

Townsend, P. (1957) *The Family Life of Old People*. London: Routledge & Kegan Paul.

Townsend, P. (1962) *The Last Refuge*. London: Routledge & Kegan Paul.

Townsend, P. (1981) 'The structured dependency of the elderly: the creation of social policy in the twentieth century', *Ageing and Society*, 1 (1): 5–28.

Townsend, P. (1986) 'Ageism and social policy', in C. Phillipson and A. Walker (eds), *Ageing and Social Policy*. Aldershot: Gower. pp. 15–44.

Townsend, P. and Wedderburn, D. (1965) *The Aged in the Welfare State*. London: Bell.

Trinder, C., Hulme, G. and McCarthy, U. (1992) *Employment: The Role of Work in the Third Age*. London: Public Finance Foundation.

Tuckman, J. and Lorge, I. (1952) 'Retirement practices in business and industry', *Journal of Gerontology*, 7: 77–86.

Tuft, N. (1982) 'Polypharmacy rules but pill pushing amongst pensioners isn't OK', *New Age*, issue no. 19: 14–16.

Tunstall, J. (1966) *Old and Alone*. London: Routledge & Kegan Paul.

Turner, B. (1989) 'Ageing, status politics and sociological theory', *British Journal of Sociology*, 40 (4): 588–606.

Turner, P., Dale, I. and Hurst, C. (1992) 'Training – a key to the future', *Employment Gazette*, August: 379–85.

Ungerson, C. (1987) *Policy is Personal: Sex, Gender and Informal Care*. London: Tavistock Books.

Vincent, J. (1995) *Inequality and Old Age*. London: UCL Press.

Waerness, K. (1989) 'Dependency in the welfare state', in M. Bulmer, J. Lewis and D. Piachaud (eds), *The Goals of Social Policy*. London: Unwin Hyman.

Walker, A. (1980) 'The social creation of poverty and dependency in old age', *Journal of Social Policy*, 9 (1): 45–75.

Walker, A. (1981) 'Towards a political economy of old age', *Ageing and Society*, 1 (1): 73–94.

Walker, A. (1986) 'Pensions and the production of poverty in old age', in A. Walker and C. Phillipson (eds), *Ageing and Social Policy.* Aldershot: Gower. pp. 184–216.

Walker, A. (1989) 'The social division of early retirement', in M. Jefferys (ed.), *Growing Old in the Twentieth Century.* London: Routledge.

Walker, A. (1993) 'Poverty and inequality in old age', in J. Bond, P. Coleman and S. Peace (eds), *Ageing and Society: An Introduction to Social Gerontology.* London: Sage. pp. 280–303.

Walker, A. (1995) *Half a Century of Promises.* London: Counsel and Care.

Walker, A. (ed.) (1996) *The New Generational Contract: Intergenerational Relations, Old Age and Welfare.* London: UCL Press.

Walker, A. and Maltby, T. (1997) *Ageing Europe.* Buckingham: Open University Press.

Walker, R. and Huby, M. (1989) 'Escaping financial dependency in old age', *Ageing and Society,* 9 (1): 17–42.

Wall, R. (1992) 'Relationships between the generations in British families past and present', in C. Marsh and S. Arber (eds), *Families and Households.* London: Macmillan.

Ward, P. (1996) *The Great British Pensions Robbery.* Preston: Waterfall Books.

Warnes, A.M. (1993) 'Being old, old people and the burdens of burden', *Ageing and Society,* 13 (3): 297–339.

Watson, G. (1994) 'The flexible workforce and patterns of working hours in the UK', *Employment Gazette,* July: 239–48.

Welford, A.T. (1958) *Ageing and Human Skill.* London: Oxford University Press for the Nuffield Foundation.

Welford, A.T. (1976) 'Thirty years of psychological research on age and work', *Journal of Occupational Psychology,* 49 (3): 129–38.

Wenger, G.C. (1984) *The Supportive Network.* George Allen & Unwin.

Wermel, M.T. and Beidemann, G.M. (1961) *Retirement Preparation Programs: A Study of Company Responsibilities.* Pasadena, CA: California Institute of Technology, Industrial Relations Section.

West, P., Illsley, R. and Kelman, H. (1984) 'Public preferences for the care of dependency groups', *Social Science and Medicine,* 18: 417–46.

Whitehouse, E. and Wolf, M. (1997) 'State retirement plan', *Financial Times,* 6 March, p. 27.

Witherspoon, S. and Taylor, B. (1990) *British Social Attitudes 1989 Survey: A Report for the Employment Department.* London: Social and Community Planning Research.

World Bank (1994) *Averting the Old Age Crisis.* Oxford: Oxford University Press.

Young, M. and Schuller, T. (1991) *Life After Work: The Arrival of the Ageless Society.* London: HarperCollins.

INDEX